D0407413

WHY O LORD?

WHY O LORD?

The Inner Meaning of Suffering

CARLO CARRETTO

Translated by ROBERT R. BARR

ORBIS BOOKS
Maryknoll, New York 10545

The Catholic Foreign Mission Society of America (Maryknoll) recruits and trains people for overseas missionary service. Through Orbis Books Maryknoll aims to foster the international dialogue that is essential to mission. The books published, however, reflect the opinions of their authors and are not meant to represent the official position of the society.

Originally published in Italian as *Perché Signore? Il Dolore: Segreto Nascosto nei Secoli* © Editrice Morcelliana, Brescia 1985

English translation copyright © 1986 by Orbis Books, Maryknoll, NY 10545
All rights reserved
Typeset in Great Britain and printed and bound in the United States of America

Library of Congress Cataloging-in-Publication Data

Carretto, Carlo.
  Why O Lord?

  Translation of: Perche Signore?
  1. Suffering—Religious aspects—Christianity.
I. Title.
BT732.7.C3613   1986   231′.8   85-29874
ISBN 0-88344-224-8
ISBN 0-88344-222-1 (pbk.)

Contents

Acknowledgements

Scripture quotations, taken from the Jerusalem Bible © 1966, 1967, 1968 Darton, Longman and Todd Ltd, and Doubleday and Company Inc., are reproduced by permission of the publishers.

1 A Little Story

Here I am in the yard behind one of the group homes organized by Chiesa-Mondo, 'Church and World', in Catania. Volunteers live here, filled with generosity and dreams, and with them live handicapped people of every sort.

Today the community has opened its doors to all its friends from town. To afford a bit of respite from the sun three tents have been erected covering every inch of available space.

Under the great canvas roofs I see a jumble of wheelchairs, sticks, and deck chairs.

Behold the sufferers' convention.

The scirocco blows with all its oppressive fidgety tension, and even Etna sits under a patchy unpleasant vapour. A thread of smoke darker than the crater of the volcano rises as though from a white scar: the last snow to linger on the fiery mountain.

My handicapped sisters and brothers have heard I am planning to write a book about suffering and death, and have asked if we could discuss those matters together.

One could hardly ask for an audience more in tune with the subject. Or more likely to make me keep quiet, gently reminding me that talk is all very well, but pain, when you can see it and feel it yourself, is another thing altogether.

The gaze of all those around me is full of kindness.

No one can look quite so kindly at you as the poor when you take an interest in them.

Or more expectantly.

It is not easy to talk to someone who is suffering. It may not even be the right thing to do.

Silence may be more appropriate.

1

But it was their idea that I should speak. They are the ones who invited me.

And I accepted. Only I didn't think there would be so many of them!

The presence of the Church and World volunteers is really something special. It gives you a sudden sense of sweetness. It helps you hope.

It's not a pretty sight, someone with cerebral palsy or paralysis, with all those jerky twisted movements, but the sight of those volunteers lovingly helping them is stupendous. Now, if it wasn't for the first there wouldn't be the second; and the sufferings of the first are material for understanding for the second.

I search within myself looking for a way to begin. And I realize that I have a stick in my hand – my own walking-stick.

Suddenly, as if for the first time in my life, I feel that I too am one of the 'handicapped'. Now I have the courage to begin.

Over the heads of the assembly I lift the stick which has supported me for nearly thirty years. And I begin.

My dear handicapped friends: today I realize that I too am one of you.

This is the first time I have realized it.

I had never felt I was one of you. You have shown me that I am, and that is the only thing that has given me the courage to speak.

Listen.

I am going to tell you part of the story of this stick that I have been using for so many years, which has become so much a part of me that I forget I have it.

I'd gone off to Africa and joined the novitiate of the Little Brothers of Jesus at El Abiodh in Algeria.

I went to the Little Brothers of Father de Foucauld in response to a call to consecration heard in my heart and requiring a clear answer from me.

The idea of giving myself to the last and least of the earth, the poorest of the poor – the thought of merging myself in the dough of the world as living leaven – attracted me.

I wanted to devote my existence to others and I wanted to do it where the going would be tough. The desert would be the perfect place, I thought. 'Present to God, and present to people', was the way the great mystic of the Sahara, Charles de Foucauld, put it and I wanted to embody those two tensions at unity in a life where contemplation and action went hand in hand.

And there in the novitiate of the Little Brothers I began to dream, and dream, and dream.

Do you know what I dreamed about?

I dreamed about becoming a Little Brother and living the Gospel among men and women who had need of me and my witness.

And who were these brothers and sisters of mine, in my dream?

Whenever we think of 'others' we have no choice but to limit the picture in our mind, and narrow it down to some particular group of people, depending on our experience, and especially depending on our feelings.

One of us will think of the Chinese and say, 'I'll devote myself to the Chinese.'

Someone else thinks of the poor of the third world with their starving babies, the peasants of Latin America, and decides, 'I'll devote myself to them.'

One of my fellow novices told me he wanted to sneak into a country behind the Iron Curtain and devote himself to the victims of atheistic propaganda.

Another one told me he would go to Hong Kong to work to build a Christianity that would be equal to face the problems of China when Hong Kong becomes part of China again.

Do you know what I wanted to do?

I was dreaming too and plans were taking shape in my heart and mind.

My dream was to go to the Alps and live with the Alpine rescue teams up on the Matterhorn, and go with them to help people caught in storms.

Dreams don't happen by accident.

All my life I had been a mountain-climber.

I'd been captain of an Alpine team, and the mountains were my passion.

I wanted to devote my passion to my fellow beings caught in the snows.

I wanted to be brother to Alpine guides and devote to their work, which is certainly not easy, my prayers and my service, as Jesus inspired me.

But I was only dreaming.

Do you know what happened to me in the middle of my dream?

I had to go on a 600 kilometre hike through the Khaloua desert from El Abiodh.

I was not in very good condition and a male nurse, my friend, who took good care of me was concerned. 'I'll give you some shots,' he said. 'You'll see, they'll keep you going.'

'Fine,' I said.

And with the best of intentions my friend stuck a needle in my thigh and injected me with a paralysing poison. In less than twenty-four hours my leg was useless.

He had made a mistake.

He'd used the wrong vial.

It was stupid, but I would not say the nurse had been at fault except in the sense that he was impulsive and careless.

I didn't complain then, and I tried to keep cheerful if only to help the nurse whose fault it was not to go out of his mind. He was not as emotionally stable as I was.

I was paralysed for life.

As soon as I felt a little better I started thinking things over. What about my dream now? What about the Alpine rescue team?

Goodbye dream. Farewell any hope of ever climbing the Matterhorn.

Suddenly I felt cheated.

How could I have been betrayed in this way?

I'd come to Africa to become a Little Brother.

I'd wanted to devote myself to people dying in snowstorms, I wanted to save them. Had I been wrong to want that?

What a perfectly miserable state of affairs!

How could the God I wanted to serve not reach out his hand when I needed him?

Why didn't he step in and stop such a simple, stupid mistake?

Why didn't he help me? Why did he let . . .

Sisters and brothers, let's stop for a moment. Let each of us think of our own suffering, our own trouble, our own paralysis, our own story.

What am I doing here?

How did I get in this wheelchair?

What am I doing with this crutch?

How comes it that I can't sleep at night?

How did I ever marry such a man, and then he abandons me to boot?

Why did that beam have to fall on me in the earthquake and crush my arm?

Why am I alone? What's wrong with just wanting to get married? And now there's no hope.

Why can't I draw just one easy breath of air?

Is someone else to blame for all this?

Or worse, is it because I'm so disordered inside?

And then, why does God, this so-called God, permit things like this?

Why doesn't he step in in time?

Why did he just stand and watch while some idiot wretch beat me within an inch of my life and now I'll never be able to walk again?

Why didn't he make Herod die before he could carry out the slaughter in Bethlehem because Jesus was a thorn in his side?

Why didn't he step in and stop that storm blowing my hut away where I lived on the shore as a poor fisherman, as poor as Jesus himself?

Does this God exist or not?

Well, if he does, why doesn't he act, why doesn't he make an exception for me?

Here I came to serve him, and all he seems to do is mock me and let me turn into a cripple.

I thought it was a good idea to devote myself, as a mountaineer, to my fellow beings freezing to death in the snow!

And now what? What am I to do now?

Not join the Alpine rescue team, that's sure!

So he's really switched things on me! Or – could it be up to me to change plans?

Could be.

Thirty years have passed since then – thirty years since my dream went wrong.

Now here I am in front of you, and you have your dreams too, or have had them. And I can tell you something.

That mistaken injection that paralysed my leg was not a stroke of bad luck. It was a grace.

Let's be precise. There's no point in pious platitudes.

It was bad luck, yes. It was a misfortune. But God turned it into a grace.

I had a useless leg. I could not climb. So I got a jeep and became a meteorologist.

Through no wish of my own, there I was where I belonged: in the desert.

Instead of trudging through the snow I trudged through the sand.

Instead of mountain passes I came to know caravan routes. Instead of chamois I saw gazelles.

Life suddenly appeared to me as it was, an immense personal exodus. Now I saw the desert as an extraordinary environment of silence and prayer.

My crippled leg helped me to 'stand firm' (Jas 1:12).

I the runner – now stood firm.

I who'd always tried to do two things at once – now I stood firm.

No doubt about it, it was a plus.

Deep down inside I began to understand that I hadn't been cheated.

Misfortune had thrust me upon new paths.

Brothers and sisters before me with your misfortunes, I testify to you of one thing only.

Today, thirty years after the incident that paralysed my leg, I don't say it wasn't a misfortune.

I only say that God was able to transform it into a grace.

I have experienced in my flesh what Augustine says: 'God permits evil, so as to transform it into a greater good.'

God loves his children, and when he sees that someone or something has hurt them, what imagination he has – to transform the evil into good, inactivity into contemplation, the cry of pain into a prayer, grief into an act of love!

I know I'm only a child, telling you these things.

Smart people don't tell you. They're embarrassed.

Well, I'm going to come right out and tell you.

I've found no other answer to my pain.

And I know it by experience. You can be happy with a crippled leg. Very happy.

In my experience the wounds of poverty and suffering produce a special, very precious, very sweet honey.

It's the honey of the Beatitudes proclaimed by Jesus in the Sermon on the Mount.

I have tasted this honey and have become convinced of the rationality of the Gospel, of the reasons for so many mysterious things.

I have been convinced by experience.

I am not going to reason with you. I am going to speak to you from experience.

I have come to believe in God through experience, and I always say: I believe in God because I know him.

And from suffering too.

There is still plenty of room for mystery. And it is right that this should be so, to educate us in humility, which is so important in our relationship with the Absolute that is God. But the thickest cloak that weighed on my misery and my blindness God has torn away, and the nakedness of my wounded flesh has helped me to recognize, out beyond the veil of mystery, the nakedness of God.

Only then, startled by joy, did I know the truth, that the encounter with him the Eternal is possible. And that it is stupendous.

I want to try to tell you something about suffering and about death. But I don't want to make a fool of myself.

I know what it means to talk to the suffering and I know

too that God alone, and Christ who died for us, are worthy to 'break the seals' of the book of life (Rev. 5:2–5).

It will be the babbling of a baby, this babbling of mine, as I try to read a mystery in faith and hope rather than in wisdom and culture.

It will be the undertaking of someone who has had the great joy of believing in the Father, of knowing his Son Jesus, and of hearing the voice of the Spirit that comes like the wind pounding on the doors of Jerusalem, and of your soul, crying with boundless gladness, 'I am here!'

I am here, to be with you. I am here, to walk with you. I am here, to love you.

Be quiet and listen.

2 The Mysterious Parable of Life

Long before Jesus told his parables to help us understand things, God the Father had told one of cosmic dimensions and as deep as the abyss: the parable of life.

His parable embraced everything visible and invisible, and instead of being expressed in words was expressed in reality – with things as they are.

The listener was immersed in this parable without any possibility of escape, for its 'words' were made of things themselves and these could in no way be denied.

'Who can gainsay the sun?' asks the sundial indicating the visible passing hour.

When the sky speaks – above your head with its billions of stars; and the earth you tread speaks – the sensible basis of living experience: how can you escape logic which surrounds you?

How can you ignore the harmony and beauty of things, or disregard the energy and power of storms and earthquakes?

How can you escape the 'absent presence' of a secret entity, the designer of a creative will and indisputable unity, of which you yourself are aware of being a part?

Call him the Architect of the world, call him Being, the Unmoved Mover; call him what you will: you cannot live long without feeling a need to reckon with him, without thinking about him, without falling in love with him even before you properly know him.

There is no escape.

If there is any doubt about him, it is about his *modus procedendi*; why he does things the way he does, and especially why he is so silent: why his presence is so mysterious and dark, even though all things speak of him.

All things.

No, I cannot doubt that everything is the expression of his invisibility, his 'presence ever-present'.

Yes, there is a cloak about his nakedness, yes he is wrapped in mystery, but that veil cannot conceal his astonishing, extra-ordinarily transparent shapes.

If creation is like a woman's swelling womb, the child within – the human being – cannot but await with impatience the bursting of the waters, to look at last on the face of its begetter.

If the reality in which God has placed human beings is the garden of Eden, which they are to cultivate and tend, this garden is itself a sufficient initiation into the experience which ought ultimately to lead them to the fullness of truth.

Even if the garden happens to be the desert, the creature has the testimony of the stars to ripen hope and foster growth.

Only wait.

Of course, waiting is not easy and haste is ever the sin of Adam.

One thing is certain: we are on earth as in a huge space where everything is light and dark at the same time, where everything is the sign of an invisible presence, and where a continual challenge comes from the splendid vault out-stretched above in its astronomical distances.

Inaccessible far-away things question us endlessly, oblige us to look up at those luminous specks like starry holes piercing the black vault, which seem to say that there, above, is the repose we seek.

How often have I known that living picture in the desert night of the Sahara!

How often, lying wrapped in a blanket on the sand, have I passed hour after hour gazing at a starry dome ceaselessly speaking to me, questioning me, helping me to find my bearings in the dark!

Why do we live?

Why do things come to be?

Why do I plod along like a wandering shepherd?

Why this vast silence?

Why do the stars look down as though indifferent to our suffering?

Withal, one thing is certain: this light, the sign of the truth we seek and the means by which we may catch a glimpse of it, has not got its roots on earth.

Light comes from up there, it comes from something stretching above me, something transcending me, something preceding me.

You can actually see this, physically.

Like it or not, the explanation I seek is not here on earth, though I may look for it here.

The earth goes on rotating on its axis, day after day, season after season, millennium after millennium, and vouchsafes no final answer to my justified questioning.

And if I try to immerse myself in work which interests me and gives a sense of achieving something with my effort and intelligence, why does the question continually recur: 'For all his toil, his toil under the sun, what does man gain by it?' (Eccles 1:3)

And if I marry and settle down so as not to feel so alone, the fact of death taking away my wife, or robbing me of my children before they can manage on their own, embitters my already harsh path.

No, a thousand times no!

The mystery is there and I cannot escape it. The mystery is there and I cannot avoid it. The mystery is there and I cannot laugh it off.

Not even the pervading sadness of Ecclesiastes' song is any consolation:

Vanity of vanities, Qoheleth says.
   Vanity of vanities. All is vanity!
For all his toil, his toil under the sun,
   what does man gain by it?
A generation goes, a generation comes,
   yet the earth stands firm for ever.

The sun rises, the sun sets; then to its place
   it speeds and there it rises.
Southward goes the wind, then turns to the north;
   it turns and turns again; back then
   to its circling goes the wind.
Into the sea all the rivers go, and yet
   the sea is never filled,
   and still to their goal the rivers go.
All things are wearisome. No man can say
   that eyes have not had enough of seeing,
   ears their fill of hearing.   (Eccles 1:2–8)

And he concludes: 'What was will be again; what has been done will be done again; and there is nothing new under the sun.' (Eccles 1:9) But that is scarcely an answer to my problem or to my need for truth.

The sacred writer then continues, swept along by his dramatic muse:

There is a season for everything, a time for every occupation under heaven:

A time for giving birth,
a time for dying;
a time for planting,
a time for uprooting what has been planted.
A time for killing,
a time for healing;
a time for knocking down,
a time for building.
A time for tears,
a time for laughter;
a time for mourning,
a time for dancing.
A time for throwing stones away,
a time for gathering them up;
a time for embracing,
a time to refrain from embracing.
A time for searching,

a time for losing;
a time for keeping,
a time for throwing away.
A time for tearing,
a time for sewing;
a time for keeping silent,
a time for speaking.
A time for living,
a time for hating;
a time for war,
a time for peace.   (Eccles 3:1–8)

How can I be satisfied with this? Poetry will not do.

Ecclesiastes' thoughts are more of a spur impelling me to look even harder for light.

And the light comes from 'up there'. 'Up there', then, is where I must seek it.

Of course, 'up there' is relative, merely relative. In fact it is inaccurate: baby language.

It is not a geographical or cosmic or ideological 'up there'. It is a sign: to explain things invisible.

In God the Absolute 'up there' and 'down here' are the same place. They embrace centre and periphery, visible and invisible, all and nothing, generator and generated, Father (himself) and child (me the human being).

All is unity, and in this unity I find the response I seek. Nothing can be foreign to his infinite rationality, his incalculable might, his perfect logic, his will, his love, his invisible visibility.

His mystery, of course, abides and I cannot escape that in my quest, but it fills all space and is enveloped in a single absolute, comprehensive, eternal answer.

If I call the 'up there' God and the 'down here' human beings – are they separate or one? Are they part of the same reality or not?

After all: what am I without him?

But I can carry this logic further and ask, 'What is he without me?'

True, without him I feel myself to be nothing, in darkness, in the void. Then how would he feel without me?

A baby cannot live without the mother who gave it life. But how can a mother live without the fruit of her intellect and womb?

I know that he is as indispensable to me as life and light. But experience has taught me to suspect that I too am indispensable to him as the fruit of his love.

Certainly I can do no less than look for him. Equally certainly he must be looking for me.

I can feel it.

And perhaps in the very search lies the beginning of the answer.

The search for each other is called love, communication, talking, listening, prayer, song, cry, waiting, embrace, banquet.

Jesus called it a kingdom: the kingdom of heaven.

He said:

The kingdom of heaven is like a treasure hidden in a field (Matt. 13:44).

The kingdom of heaven may be compared to a man who sowed good seed (Matt. 13:24).

The kingdom of heaven is like a mustard seed (Matt. 13:31).

The kingdom of heaven is like a dragnet cast into the sea (Matt. 13:47).

The kingdom of heaven is like a landowner going out at daybreak to hire workers (Matt. 20:1).

The kingdom of heaven will be like this: Ten bridesmaids took their lamps and went to meet the bridegroom (Matt. 25:1).

The kingdom of heaven may be compared to a king who gave a feast for his son's wedding (Matt. 22:2).

In this astonishing image of the kingdom we have everything.

There is life with its excitement, there is encounter, there is becoming, maturity born of responsibility, development and how it comes about; there is fullness, there is joy, there is the eternal, the human, punishment and reward: there is hope, there is love.

Truly this is the final unshakable kingdom with its logic matured in trial and responsibility, with its struggles, dreams, its beginning and its end.

The Hebrews envisaged it as a covenant between God and the human being. The mystics imagined it as a marriage; the evangelists as an eternal banquet.

Jesus himself called it blessedness.

And all of them saw it as peace, joy and fullness.

Certainly seen this way things are easy, and at last I feel contented, a smile begins to come to my face.

But . . . But . . .

In the street I hear: 'Why all this pain? Why do the innocent suffer? Why must we die?'

The sky that momentarily looked so bright has now gone black.

Thick clouds rise over my restricted human horizon, poor weak fearful creature that I am!

And I am confounded.

It is true. There is so much suffering. And I have every right to wonder why.

In fact: why evil?

Why gaols? Why asylums? Why wars?

O the scream of all the sick!

O the slow agony of all the dying!

O the cold sweat of those in agony!

And I am back where I started. But this time I am left only with silence.

To talk about this to someone tortured by cancer, or shredded alive in a motor accident which destroyed life's hopes in an instant, becomes presumption.

Who am I to give you any sort of answer?

And yet when you gaze at me with your eyes full of terror and tears what am I to say to you?

Do you even want me to speak?

Have you still got the strength to hear me in your torment?

Brothers and sisters, I do not know what to say to you.

I have already passed the seventy years the psalmist allots to human life.

I stop talking, sit down beside you and with no right but that of someone who has suffered a little, like you, I say: The luckiest thing that ever happened to me in my life was getting to know God.

Yes, I honestly mean it. I tell you this in the Spirit: I know God. I've begun to get to know him.

In fact – as I always tell my friends – I believe in God because I know him.

Try and follow my line of reasoning for a moment.

Grit your teeth if you are in pain, but listen to what I am going to say.

As long as I have known God I have never known him to let me down.

I know that he cannot deceive me. This is my strength.

Knowledge of him has led me to trust in him.

I have this experience within me; nothing can abolish it.

I trust in him.

I trust in him even when my faith is put to the test and I understand nothing.

I trust in him even when my horizon is dark, arid and painful.

I may say that this confidence is the outcome of seventy years on the road.

I no longer remember what being a religious means. I no longer remember whether I am sinful or virtuous. I am no longer interested in such things.

One thing, though, I do remember: that I can trust myself to him. I know that he is not the kind to make fun of me. I know that he is faithful.

Yes, he is faithful.

Now if he is faithful he will explain to me the things that at present I cannot grasp.

He will explain the reason for suffering, the reason for death, the reason for evil.

A parent does not desert a child.

A friend does not betray a friend.

And he is both my father and my friend.

I tell you this from direct experience.

I am not telling you this only in faith, which is one of his gifts. I am telling you from experience, which is our acquisition, the outcome of our life's journey.

I cannot always understand why he does this or that. But I know from experience that he does well.

I trust him.

And if there is pain in the world, I know from experience that he knows there is, and knows how to transform it into light, freedom and bliss.

Yes, into bliss. It may seem quite a task! If not downright ridiculous.

How can you say that those who weep are blessed?

And yet blessed is what he called them.

Read the Beatitudes. Now go ahead and say it, he won't be offended: These are the words of a madman, or else of someone holding something back.

I would say, both. He is mad, but mad with love.

And as far as holding something back is concerned I can have no doubt of that.

He conceals things.

He conceals things when he is ready but we cannot bear them; more especially he conceals them to ask us for the only things he cannot otherwise get: love and trust.

He is in love with the trust that we can repose in him.

Nothing gives him greater joy than that act of trust which makes possible the loving relationship he yearns to establish with us.

This is the greatest gift that we as creatures can give him.

There is no greater act of love than that of letting go in the dark and falling into the arms of our lover with total abandon; offering all for love.

Listen to what Father de Foucauld said in the desert.

He really understood.

Father,
I abandon myself into your hands;
do with me what you will.
Whatever you may do, I thank you:
I am ready for all, I accept all.
Let only your will be done in me,
and in all your creatures.
I wish no more than this, O Lord.
Into your hands I commend my soul;
I offer it to you with all the love of my heart,
for I love you, Lord, and so need to give myself,
to surrender myself into your hands, without reserve,
and with boundless confidence,
for you are my Father.

That is how to pray when you are suffering. That is how
to believe in God.

3 Why, Lord?

When you are suffering, in flesh or in spirit, the natural response is to weep.

And what a lot of weeping there is!

If we could gather it all in one place it would fill a sea, a great ocean.

Then, when our eyes are dry for an instant, we ask, why?

Why, Lord, all this weeping?

The answer does not come easily.

And again we begin to weep and our thoughts become all tangled and even more sorrowful, and we stumble about like wounded birds.

Then we start again asking: why?

Why?

Anyone who suffers a great deal says eventually, like Job: 'May the day perish when I was born, and the night that told of a boy conceived.' (Job 3:3)

Under the heavy hand of suffering we can fail to grasp the reason for life, and curse life as a hopeless misfortune.

That is the pit of the abyss and total darkness where the gleam of faith has gone out altogether.

But the matter is much more complex. Even if I am screaming I realize that my words are senseless. A way of releasing pressure. Not meant to produce an answer.

Then again the weeping begins, and swells the level of the great sea of suffering.

Finally in the depths of the abyss a tiny glimmer of hope blossoms, as if the pain we experience has generated a logic until now concealed.

It is impossible for all this not to have a meaning. It is

19

impossible that he who made heaven and earth has not also given a reason for the darkness swallowing me up in the heavy cloak of suffering!

Indeed God himself undertakes to answer me, as if to stop my tongue:

> Where were you when I laid the earth's foundations?
>   Tell me, since you are so well-informed!
> Who decided the dimensions of it, do you know?
>   Or who stretched the measuring line across it?
> What supports its pillars at their bases?
>   Who laid its cornerstone
> when all the stars of the morning were singing with joy,
>   and the Sons of God in chorus were chanting praise?
> Who pent up the sea behind closed doors
>   when it leapt tumultuous out of the womb,
> when I wrapped it in a robe of mist
>   and made black clouds its swaddling bands;
> when I marked the bounds it was not to cross
>   and made it fast with a bolted gate?
> Come thus far, I said, and no farther:
>   here your proud waves shall break.　　　(Job 38:4–11)

And as if that were not enough, God goes on:

> Have you journeyed all the way to the sources of the sea,
>   or walked where the Abyss is deepest?
> Have you been shown the gates of Death
>   or met the janitors of Shadowland?
> Have you an inkling of the extent of the earth?
>   Tell me all about it if you have!
> Which is the way to the home of the light,
>   and where does darkness live?
> You could then show them the way to their proper places,
>   or put them on the path to where they live!
>
>   　　　　　　　　　　　　　　　　　(Job 38:16–20)

This is his way of talking and produces an answering echo

in me, since his way is very much like my way, putting me on very familiar ground.

I cannot deny the visible which stands before me. I cannot deny the created universe.

I cannot fail to see the marvel of the flowers, the power of the sea, the logic of a computer, the boundless depth of space.

I cannot say, 'This is mere accident.'

The discourse of signs puts me to the question. The signs are not here by accident; they are part of reality.

Ever since I was a child I have been assimilating this theology of signs, signs crowding on me from all sides with indisputable beauty, harmony, strength and clarity.

The sea is there and I see it, the sky is there and I admire it, heat is there and I feel it, food is there and I taste it.

I cannot remain indifferent. The signs, nature and space, are the open pages of a book which, like it or not, I must be able to read.

And as I read I think; and my thought is ever directed towards an unknown invisible centre, present everywhere, extraordinarily fascinating; the other-than-I, the silent answer to my question: the Absolute.

I imagine him to be like a seeing eye, a knowing being, a willing will. Exodus has defined him as 'I Am who I Am' (Exod. 3:14). The East likes to call him Universal Harmony. Islam salutes him as the Mighty, the Glorified, the Invisible, the Majestic, the Witness. Jesus calls him Father.

But who can know the whole mystery expressed in these words which we pronounce?

Now once more I weep, for the pain has become unbearable and these signs – no more than words – are not enough to soothe me and give an adequate response.

The mystery abides.

The most I can do is to strive to find comfort in the words which by the very strength of their logic comforted Job: 'I know that you are all-powerful: what you conceive, you can perform' (Job 42:2).

And then, with him, I add oddly: 'I knew you then only by hearsay; but now, having seen you with my own eyes . . .' (Job 42:5).

Here is something new indeed. You might say that the very experience of pain has brought us something we did not have before.

With the pain comes nothing less than knowledge of the Absolute, knowledge of God. Lord, 'I knew you then only by hearsay; but now, having seen you with my own eyes . . .'

What has happened?

In experiencing suffering, what has happened in me?

Well, at least I can say that suffering has brought me 'inside things' – into the light, into matter, into laws, into cells.

What would I know of a stone had I never stubbed my toe on one?

What would I know of the seasons had I not learnt from heat and cold how to live in them?

What would I know of the pleasures of the table had I never experienced what it is to work?

Have I not learned the value of water from thirst, and the importance of good food from hunger?

And what would children mean to me if I did not make them mine through the thirst for parenthood, the joy of love, the concern to provide them with their bread, the anxiety of seeing them ill and the sorrow of knowing them to be far away?

Imagine for a moment a universe without tension – nature without agonies, a world without sweat, body without joy, loaf without the oven; a work of art without creativity, a great love without waiting.

This would be a mummified universe, a world without becoming, a wooden worm-eaten human being, a story without a twist, a baby without wonder.

It would be one great death, a life never lived, a school closed with no pupils, a heart without awareness.

And how would life be possible without awareness?

But that is easy to say.

The road is long and the secret is still hidden.

It is small consolation to eat a good meal after a hard day's work if I have just been laid off.

The joy of having my baby is not enough if I suddenly learn that she will die of leukaemia.

The harmony and power of human research says little when there is a missile pointing to the sky.

No, that is quite different.

Above all – at the bottom of my cup of life, at the end of my toil and sweat, after my dreams have been dreamt, there is a graveyard waiting for me, and worse, for those I love, from whom the mere thought of separation leaves me utterly destroyed.

The pangs of nature generating life, as though in an agony of parturition, do not completely convince me but often leave me perplexed.

There must be something else.

The secret is still hidden.

When the earth quakes and my house collapses about my ears, once again I have doubts about the logic of creation, however often I may have delighted in its wonders.

When the hospital opens its doors to receive my suffering body, in my sleepless nights it is not easy for me to feel at peace.

When I see the arrogant triumphant while the poor starve, once again I doubt the presence of a good and just God.

When I have drunk my cup of misery to the dregs and see there with failing eyes the end of my earthly days, it is not easy for me to feel cheerful.

The mystery abides, or, rather, stretches above me.

Reason no longer helps me, my heart grows dry, my strength leaves me.

In the darkness I feel that I must search elsewhere. It is not easy.

Where should I look?

I shall search in him, now that I have begun to know him by living experience.

But it is precisely when thinking about him that no answer comes.

I might even say that he himself is the difficulty.

If he is so good, why does he make me suffer?

If he can do all things, why does he leave me in my distress?

What do you want from me, God?

Why is your will different from mine?

It looks as though you are indifferent to my pain, my anguish, since you, yes, you are the one who sends me these trials.

Why, Lord?

Now that I know you, no longer by hearsay but because I have seen your face, I see that it is you who strike me!

Like Jeremiah, I too have realized this.

Listen, Lord, to what a man can say about you.

I am the man familiar with misery
    under the rod of his anger;
I am the one he has driven and forced to walk
    in darkness, and without any light.
Against me alone he turns his hand,
    again and again, all day long.

He has wasted my flesh and skin away,
    has broken my bones.
He has made a yoke for me,
    has encircled my head with weariness.
He has forced me to dwell in darkness
    with the dead of long ago.

He has walled me in; I cannot escape;
    he has made my chains heavy;
and when I call and shout,
    he shuts out my prayer.
He has blocked my ways with cut stones,
    he has obstructed my paths.

For me he has been a lurking bear,
a lion on the watch.
He has filled my paths with briars and torn me,
he has made me a thing of horror.
He has bent his bow and taken aim,
making me the target for his arrows.

In my back he has planted his darts,
the children of his quiver.
I have become the laughing-stock of my whole nation,
their butt all day long.
He has given me my fill of bitterness,
he has made me drunk with wormwood.

He has broken my teeth with gravel,
he has given me ashes for food.
My soul is shut out from peace;
I have forgotten happiness.
And now I say, 'My strength is gone,
that hope which came from Yahweh'.

Brooding on my anguish and affliction
is gall and wormwood.
My spirit ponders it continually
and sinks within me. (Lam. 3:1–20)

This ordeal is frightful.

To know from experience that God can do all things and that what he chooses to do is to let you suffer!

Because, yes he can do all things.

He can, and allowed none other than his Son to be nailed to the cross.

He can, and allows the poor to be treated like dirt and scoffed at by the mighty.

He lets the innocent suffer and the righteous die.

It is Good Friday, the hour when everyone has run away.

It is the hour of darkness.

On this day at this hour, who could understand the prophecy contained in the very death of Jesus?

No one had thought it would end like that.

The darkness of Calvary is truly the quintessence of darkness as experienced by human beings on earth and under ordeal.

My God, my God, why have you deserted me?
How far from saving me, the words I groan!
I call all day, my God, but you never answer,
all night long I call and cannot rest.   (Ps. 22:1–2)

Why, Lord?
Why, Lord?
Why?

4 The Messianic Dream

Like Job, the thinking person looks for an answer to the problem of pain.

But the loving person tries another way – the way of the dream. It is the right way for the one who has the courage of faith.

To be sure, a book about suffering more outstandingly true, human or moving than the Book of Job would be hard to find. And it is just as hard to find a dream more beautiful, more pregnant with hope, than the messianic dream.

Here the word of God sets off down a path characteristically, and none the less marvellously, designed for the least, for the believers; designed for the pure in heart and the poor in spirit; designed for dreamers.

Yes, it is called a dream.

With it the people of God are satisfied to the point of exaltation.

And a dream it is – a dream that commandeers a universe of human possibilities and seeks to transfer painful dark, persecuted, bloody reality to a new dimension where all is joy, justice and peace; and where 'there will be no more death, and no more mourning or sadness' (Rev. 21:4).

This messianic dream is the grandest hope ever conceived by mankind desiring the triumph of truth and love.

It is Utopia made living fact in the guts of those who have the courage to hope, those who feel that the world is heading for resurrection and not for chaos.

The messianic dream offers the solution to all problems, the response to all darkness, even the blackest, and the soothing away of all anxiety.

All said and done, the messianic dream is the vital support of the people of God on their journey through the desert: security in insecurity, freedom in slavery, strength under ordeal; our means of surviving the horrendous Diaspora of Babylon.

This is how the prophet proclaims it:

> . . . say to all faint hearts,
> 'Courage! Do not be afraid.
>
> 'Look, your God is coming,
> vengeance is coming,
> the retribution of God;
> he is coming to save you.'   (Isa. 35:4)

The dream begins here.

There is someone coming to save me, someone who will help me, someone to snatch me out of prison.

But not only that.

There is someone who will change things at their root, who will make new times, new things, new highways. Listen.

> Then the eyes of the blind shall be opened,
> the ears of the deaf unsealed,
> then the lame shall leap like a deer
> and the tongues of the dumb sing for joy;
>
> for water gushes in the desert,
> streams in the wasteland,
> the scorched earth becomes a lake,
> the parched land springs of water.
>
> The lairs where the jackals used to live
> become thickets of reed and papyrus . . .
>
> And through it will run a highway undefiled
> which shall be called the Sacred Way;
> the unclean may not travel by it,
> nor fools stray along it.

No lion will be there
nor any fierce beast roam about it,
but the redeemed will walk there,
for those Yahweh has ransomed shall return.

They will come to Zion shouting for joy,
everlasting joy on their faces;
joy and gladness will go with them
and sorrow and lament be ended.   (Isa. 35:5–10)

For me, who am blind and deaf and lame, this is a dream
which alters the picture of my life, thrusting me into hope,
into a reality that will be fulfilled, that will be mine forever.

Everything will be changed, even the dryness of the desert,
even the impassable roads, even sorrow and weeping.

And what does the prophet tell me, I who am so obsessed
with the sight of the suffering of innocent children, so accustomed to daily injustices and violence and wars on this deso-
late earth?

A shoot springs from the stock of Jesse,
a scion thrusts from his roots:
on him the spirit of Yahweh rests,
a spirit of wisdom and insight,
a spirit of counsel and power,
a spirit of knowledge and of the fear of Yahweh.
(The fear of Yahweh is his breath.)
He does not judge by appearances,
he gives no verdict on hearsay,
but judges the wretched with integrity,
and with equity gives a verdict for the poor of the land.
His word is a rod that strikes the ruthless,
his sentences bring death to the wicked.

Integrity is the loincloth round his waist,
faithfulness the belt about his hips.

The wolf lives with the lamb,
the panther lies down with the kid,

calf and lion cub feed together
with a little boy to lead them.
The cow and the bear make friends,
their young lie down together.
The lion eats straw like the ox.
The infant plays over the cobra's hole;
into the viper's lair
the young child puts his hand.
They do no hurt, no harm,
on all my holy mountain,
for the country is filled with the knowledge of Yahweh
as the waters swell the sea.   (Isa. 11:1–9)

There are no limits to the sweetness of this vision, the brightness of a picture filled with a dream.

Without blinking an eye what improbable things he asserts for people who are accustomed to live in endless war, and who know the wickedness of the powers that be, the pharaohs of succeeding ages!

In the days to come
the mountain of the Temple of Yahweh
shall tower above the mountains
and be lifted higher than the hills.
All the nations will stream to it,
peoples without number will come to it; and they will say:
'Come, let us go up to the mountain of Yahweh,
to the Temple of the God of Jacob
that he may teach us his ways
so that we may walk in his paths;
since the Law will go out from Zion,
and the oracle of Yahweh from Jerusalem'.

He will wield authority over the nations
and adjudicate between many peoples;
these will hammer their swords into ploughshares,
their spears into sickles.
Nation will not lift sword against nation,
there will be no more training for war.   (Isa. 2:2–4)

Yes we shall hammer our swords into ploughshares and our spears into sickles.

Dreams?

Yes, but dreams that give us life and courage, snatching us from our existential doubt which is our true sin, and offering us a different world within us which, if it were up to us, we should build in the blink of an eye.

Who is to say that 'he who made heaven and earth' (Ps. 134:3) does not have the same ideas, the same desires as we do?

And who is to say that he himself has not put the dream in our heart, suggested it, told us to journey on until we fulfil it, told us that we shall build it – that it will come one day?

Yes, it will come . . .

Meanwhile I think.

Meanwhile I dream, I feel encouraged. I breathe more easily.

And being little helps.

And being poor helps, especially if I do not waste time in useless requests.

The messianic dream is a proclamation from heaven and earth, a bridge between two banks, a tree on your parched path.

Inspiration comes from afar but you are the ones to experience it.

You receive a proclamation but it is up to you to meditate on it. It comes from the far side but becomes a reality on your side.

I believe this is the way God calls to us, educates us, accustoms us to his way of thinking.

By listening, journeying, pausing, you make the dream more definite.

I have experienced this.

Learn to taste him, get used to his logic, admire its contents.

Thousands over the centuries have slaked their thirst at this spring, thousands have found repose in the shade of this tree put by their road!

Listen.

Let the wilderness and the dry-lands exult,
let the wasteland rejoice and bloom,
let it bring forth flowers like the jonquil,
let it rejoice and sing for joy.

The glory of Lebanon is bestowed on it,
the splendour of Carmel and Sharon;
they shall see the glory of Yahweh,
the splendour of our God.

Strengthen all weary hands,
steady all trembling knees
and say to all faint hearts,
'Courage! Do not be afraid.

'Look, your God is coming,
vengeance is coming,
the retribution of God;
he is coming to save you.'   (Isa. 35:1–4)

And if one of you is weeping for the sufferings of the world,
say this:

'Console my people, console them'
says your God.
'Speak to the heart of Jerusalem
and call to her
that her time of service is ended . . .'   (Isa. 40:1–2)

And those weighed down by their past:

No need to recall the past,
no need to think about what was done before.
See, I am doing a new deed,
even now it comes to light; can you not see it?
                                              (Isa. 43:18–19)

Then with sweet faith-filled wonder the prophet sings on:

How beautiful on the mountains,
are the feet of one who brings good news,
who heralds peace, brings happiness,
proclaims salvation,
and tells Zion,
'Your God is king!'   (Isa. 52:7)

And over whom does this God reign? Where is he?
Why, he is so near; he is looking for you.

For now your creator will be your husband,
his name, Yahweh Sabaoth;
your redeemer will be the Holy One of Israel,
he is called the God of the whole earth.   (Isa. 54:5)

How wild a dream! Nor could there be any more beautiful.
Yes, God is so close to you that he calls you 'my bride'.
It would seem absurd, were it not the Word himself
speaking.
Yet it is true, and this wonderful intuition, the glory of
God's people, runs through the Bible from end to end.

Like a young man marrying a virgin,
so will the one who built you wed you . . .   (Isa. 62:5)

And in the face of fear, the creature's constant difficulty, the
prophet goes on:

for the mountains may depart,
the hills be shaken,
but my love for you will never leave you
and my covenant of peace with you will never be
   shaken . . .   (Isa. 54:10)

Of course he knows you will go on doubting and whim-
pering, 'the Lord has forgotten me' (Isa. 49:14).
And so the answer comes back like a refrain:

Does a woman forget her baby at the breast,
or fail to cherish the son of her womb?
Yet even if these forget,
I will never forget you.   (Isa. 49:15)

And he even tells you with indescribable tenderness, 'See, I have branded you on the palms of my hands' (Isa. 49:16).

What more do you want?

I shall tell you – says the Lord – not this time in a dream but in hard fact.

You shall see what I intend to do for you.

5 The Kingdom is Real: and so is our Exodus

The dream of course is just a dream, even if it is the messianic dream. But what the Gospel calls the kingdom is fact – realized in us a little at a time in all the beauty of its design, the marvel of its structures, the fertility of life and the inexhaustible loving creativity of God.

The kingdom of God is the final project of the Absolute, the end of creation, the future of the human being, the answer to people's questions and the revealing of all mysteries.

All things converge on the kingdom Christ came to announce. This is the definitive response to what we see, the meaning of the history in which we are involved, the object of our final expectation.

The kingdom is our future: heaven and earth are its space, the visible and the invisible its reality-in-becoming, God and ourselves its actualizers. The kingdom of God is at the centre of God's heart and of human awareness.

For the poor, the unimportant, the oppressed the kingdom is perfectly intelligible. For the rich, the sated, the sensual it is mysterious and not anything they want to seek.

As Jesus was to say, the kingdom of God is good news to the poor (Luke 4:18; cf. Isa. 61:1): the poor can understand what it means, though of course it is destined to come about and no power on earth can prevent it doing so.

Pride – another name of idolatry – refuses to believe in the kingdom but is constantly in collision with it, since the kingdom lies in everybody's path. The cause of the collision is always an idol embodying pride, and the word of God mocks idols, saying they have 'eyes, but never see . . . hands, but never touch, feet, but never walk' (Ps. 115:5–7).

35

To make pride see the error of its ways it has to be defeated, and all security destroyed.

There is only God!

This is the cornerstone of the kingdom.

Nothing can disturb the design, the perfection of the kingdom, nothing can change the will of God.

At the very most you can remain on the outside. But everything is so arranged that to stay outside is a continuous hell, and the anguish of loneliness will be enough to change your mind and, with all due respect, ask to be allowed to enter.

The virtue that changes your mind and teaches you to see aright is humility. And to teach you well, there is all the suffering of life and the constant vision of death to take care of that.

This is no joke.

Who can resist God?

You are certainly free to do so but there is precious little advantage in it.

I do not think resisting God for long would be feasible.

All round the kingdom which God's love has designed and willed is an 'anti-kingdom', the dominion of 'evil', of 'Satan the divider', of the 'Liar'. And it is so horrible that – if I may proffer my personal opinion – I do not think anyone would willingly choose to make it his or remain forever under its sway.

For that matter, since I know the king I can assure you that his deepest desires are those for love and peace and that he has done and will do everything to ensure that all will be saved who enter this kingdom.

Anything else would be strange indeed!

The kingdom of God is the great novelty, and its proclamation is the good news which the king's son himself has come to announce. And his testimony has cost him dear.

It was worth the price, though. By dying and rising again – by this solo event – Jesus has explained everything to us.

By dying he has explained the value of what he was

teaching us. By rising again he has removed any doubt still weighing on our heart: the fear of death.

Yes, even death could be vanquished.

He has vanquished it.

Brothers and sisters!

Perhaps the sub-title, 'The inner meaning of suffering', was what tempted you to open this book. It is the secret hidden in the ages! You have certainly grasped what it is about.

We hear so much about suffering and death, especially today with the collapse of traditional values and the temptations we all suffer against faith.

Well, the answer will be in the kingdom.

If you accept the kingdom everything is clear. If you do not accept it nothing is clear.

If the kingdom of eternal life exists suffering and death have meaning. If it does not exist there is no explanation at all.

And you can be sure of this: you will not find a solution elsewhere. You will remain in anguish and darkness.

I know I am telling you these things in faith but I have no other means of doing so.

There are no other means.

We are not autonomous on this earth.

Even at the physical level we are not autonomous. We depend entirely on a distant sun. If the sun should fail for a single week we would be plunged into icy chaotic destruction.

As the earth depends on the sun, so human beings depend on their sun. What this sun is is something I have got to find out; but I certainly depend on a sun. And it is from this sun that life comes, since my own is not sufficient in itself and I long for a life that will be eternal.

It is unthinkable that the inventor of mankind would have destined us to futile extinction.

Logic demands that he has given us a future, a becoming, a development, an exodus; and he has taught us this by ripening our awareness which is in fact the locus of our identity and the most important discovery we make.

Even as we pass through the shadows we are aware of the continuity and eternity of life.

The conventional missionary may never come. The distance may be too great and the journey too difficult.

The Holy Spirit, the creator who made heaven and earth, supplies the want. He has willed us into existence and has not left us on our own. He has taught us a daily catechism, telling us: You are eternal because you are my child. I have prepared the kingdom for you and you will be with me forever.

The proclamation of this kingdom is good news for everyone.

It is worth hearing.

But where can you hear it?

You need not go far. The hearing is within us – in the depths of each one of us.

Christ's proclamation that 'the kingdom of God is among you' (Luke 17:21) is the foundation of everything.

Long had the call been prepared and formulated in the heart of mankind.

Ever since its creation the human mind had been waiting, trying to understand like a bewildered child. How could God's call have echoed in man's head, had there been no ear to hear it? Can the bridegroom ask something of the bride when the bride does not exist? Can a parent call a child if there is no child?

It all happens as it happens with love. The yes of the one partner corresponds exactly to the yes of the other.

To have a conversation, to meet, to embrace, there must be two.

It is not very warm alone, says Wisdom; and not even the mystery of God is one of solitude. The Father loves the Son, and the Son loves the Father, and they engender love.

It is the same with the kingdom. God proclaims it and men and women accept it.

God comes knocking at the door; we are there and open the door.

Later we learn that the kingdom is a banquet and we are sitting opposite each other at the same table.

How beautiful, how simple!

God traces a design. I recognize it as exactly in accordance with the lines already in me.

'. . . the kingdom of God is among you'.

We can truly say in the matter of the kingdom that all depends on God and all depends on us.

It is a common intention.

It is a covenant.

It is a birth. The soil has been fertilized; the father has found the child.

The human being is the child and God is the Father.

That is the substance of the Gospel.

But the Father seeks concord with the child and the child can do nothing without the Father.

The kingdom of God is really an act of love, and love is only possible in reciprocal acceptance – in a yes pronounced by both.

The project becomes a project in common.

Once God became man, man became divine.

Once God prepares the banquet, man is the indispensable guest.

God's action is vain unless the human being responds.

John sees them in such union, such an inseparable entity, that he uses the example of a grapevine: 'I am the vine, you are the branches.' (John 15:5)

The visible fruit is on the branch. The branch is the human being. The invisible sap is the invisible life-giving presence of God within the human being.

'. . . cut off from me you can do nothing', says Jesus (John 15:5), proclaiming the presence of the divine within the human. But he also says to mankind, 'You are the light of the world' (Matt. 5:14), to affirm the factual importance of mankind in making the kingdom visible.

And to emphasize once for all the importance of man, matured by suffering and grown autonomous, he does not hesitate to scandalize the Temple by asserting the primacy of the human over the sacred, in the tremendous words, 'The sabbath was made for man, not man for the sabbath' (Mark 2:27); as if to establish the principle of what men and women are for God. Yes, God is truly the Other for human beings; by the same token man is truly the Other for God.

You can't go further than that.

The sacred itself, the sabbath itself, comes second.

The kingdom is fulfilled only in the liberty of love, in an unconditional choice made by two, in the reciprocal acceptance of the common project. The kingdom is not imposed. It is a choice, and just as it was an act of love on the part of God himself, so it is also an act of love on the part of the human beings who receive it.

Our option of saying no, in non-acceptance, will always remain a terrible terrifying fact, the price of freedom, and hell will ever hang over the head of whoever journeys towards the reality of love as the indispensable locus of our freedom. Freedom actually demands the threat and challenge of the unbearable scandal of hell. If there was only paradise, human beings would not be free. If there was only the door to our Father's house, we should be conditioned, and always feel we were being used, or frustrated.

In the terrifying desert of our choices – and it really is terrifying – there is both a path to the Promised Land and the possibility of returning to the slavery of Egypt.

God says in Deuteronomy: 'See, today I set before you life and prosperity, death and disaster' (Deut. 30:15). Here are good and evil. Choose.

This choice is our heritage. We have no other.

There is no escaping it, for God's love demands it of us, and our freedom must respond.

Love gives us plenty of time to answer but the hour of the answer is final.

Love will not have the bad taste to ask me for my answer at an unsuitable moment, or at a time when physical weakness conditions my responses. But he will ask me none the less.

Love has demands. And will not wait forever.

In the light of the kingdom many things start getting clearer.

My destiny is eternal.

The eternal is love.

Love is a partnership.

Partnership is a community of will.

Here I begin to understand what John says in his Gospel: 'all I have is yours and all you have is mine' (John 17:10).

God's interests are our interests and ours are God's.

But more than interests, it is a matter of tastes.

God's tastes must become our tastes.

Here lies the problem.

How can you live in the same house with someone (forever!) without the same likes and dislikes?

How can you sit at table together with different plans – or worse, opposing ones?

'I died on the cross for you and you don't move a finger for me,' Jesus would have the right to say to me. And:

'I'm faithful, I've never betrayed you. And you? Betray me is all you do.

'I love poverty. What about you? What do you love?

'I consented to be humiliated, ridiculed, defeated, while you are afraid of what others will think of you. You tremble if someone criticizes you in the paper!'

Isn't this so?

The journey is long and its name is exodus.

The exodus is the journey made by human beings to learn God's tastes by experience.

It is God's school, the apprenticeship of the kingdom, the child's growing up to become like the parent.

All life is an exodus and I think (again, this is only my personal opinion) that this exodus does not end with a car accident or a sudden heart attack or a bullet from some nasty little thug.

No way! Our exodus is much longer than the time spent under the sun here on earth – much longer.

Our exodus embraces vaster universes.

On earth an individual barely has time to be born, like a grass seed producing a shoot, say a centimetre long. Then comes physical death interrupting our earthly experience, while the shoot keeps growing, say to the height of a metre. Then there is the ear which to me represents the fullness of the kingdom, the harvest to be gathered into the barn, as the Gospel says.

If harvest came when the seed was sprouting where should we be?

Which of us would reach the maturity of Christ?

To be gathered into the Father's barn do we not need the 'fullness of Christ' (cf. Eph. 4:13)?

To sit down at table with him, must we not have the same desires as him?

> His state was divine,
> yet he did not cling
> to his equality with God
> but emptied himself
> to assume the condition of a slave,
> and became as men are;
> and being as all men are,
> he was humbler yet,
> even to accepting death,
> death on a cross.
>
>   (Phil. 2:6–8)

No, we shall not enter the kingdom until we have accepted the demands of love to the hilt, until we have desired to die for love of all our fellow men, until we have mounted the cross and ideally shed our last drop of blood!

And you want to enter the kingdom with your thoughts greedily revolving round the money left in your cashbox, on your cheque-book still on the table, with your clothes still smelling of tobacco, with your envelope of cocaine in your pocket?

Or, worse, with hatred for your landlord or dislike of your husband in your heart?

Before long the kingdom would grow ugly and the eternal banquet repulsive.

No my sisters, no, brothers, believe me: the exodus begins when you receive baptism, normally baptism with water; and ends when you are baptized with your own blood – every last drop of it.

As happened to Jesus.

What convinced me that our exodus lasts longer than our

time spent on earth, that it goes on much longer after physical death, was my reading of the works of St John of the Cross.

This Spanish mystic, this incredible individual, this most courageous of Christians, describes in his books the *way* we travel, and describes it so well and so clearly that as you read it you say to yourself, 'This fellow's speaking from experience. He isn't making any of this up.'

And what did he find along the way?

He found liberation which is precisely the theme of the whole exodus.

When we come out of Egypt we are called by God to freedom, total freedom, true freedom, eternal freedom.

But in order to become free – what a task, what a struggle, what a purging!

Liberation from the clutches of the senses is no small thing for sensual creatures like us.

To reach the 'night of the senses' – the time when we become rulers of our passions and are able to resist the extravagances of taste and physical pleasure – that takes some fasting!

But this is nothing yet. This is only the beginning – baby stuff, you might say.

There's more to come!

There is another darker, much more painful night.

It is the 'night of the soul', the night in which we chatter-boxes have to learn to keep still.

We who are so ready to ask for things – now we shall not dare to ask.

We fall silent, thunderstruck with the grandeur that confronts us: God.

We fall silent, in love with him.

It was Jesus himself who said, 'When that day comes, you will not ask me any questions.' (John 16:23)

The night of the spirit is the mature ability of the human being to love God in the dark, to accept the design even without seeing it, to bear the distance without complaining, even when love thrusts us towards him until we writhe with longing.

The suffering is terrible and St John of the Cross makes no attempt to conceal it.

But this is not yet all. So far, along the way only the purification of faith and hope has been accomplished.

Now to complete the journey – the flight, as the Spanish mystic would say – love must be purified and transformed into charity.

What does this mean?

It is simple.

It means imitating Jesus on the road to Jerusalem.

Every situation must be reversed.

I who have used Jerusalem for my pleasures must sacrifice my pleasures for Jerusalem.

I who have made use of others for my amusement must make my life the tool of my fellow men.

I who have been so afraid to suffer must accept Calvary with Jesus.

Like Jesus.

My exodus does not end when I die in my bed, but when I die on the cross of Christ.

Now *there* is something to fear. And we want to shout, 'No one can go that far!'

And we would be right. But we know that the miracle worker is love itself.

God is God and he is the God of the impossible.

6 The Real Secret

That God exists is no secret. It is clear to see!

That the human being is eternal is no secret. It's in the logic of things!

That God is good is no secret. It is the experience of every ready heart.

That God is beautiful is no secret. It is written on every flower, on the sea and on the mountains.

That God is immense is no secret. All you have to do is look at the universe.

That God is the memory of the world is no secret. All you have to do is glance at a computer.

That God is near is no secret. You only need to look at a couple on their honeymoon, or a hen with her chicks, or two friends talking, or an expectant mother.

But then, where is the secret?

Here it is: God is a crucified God.

God is the God who allows himself to be defeated, God is the God who has revealed himself in the poor. God is the God who has washed my feet, God is Jesus of Nazareth.

We were not accustomed to a God like this.

In our childhood, the childhood of the people of God, we sought a mighty God, a God who would solve problems, a God who would eliminate the wicked, a God who would conquer enemies in a way that everyone could see.

And instead?

He appeared as a baby. He presented himself as a poor worker, not using his divinity to gain his bread.

He struck no alliances with the mighty to lord it over peoples.

He refused to leap from the pinnacle of the Temple, to work the inappropriate miracles we were expecting to make us feel more secure.

And when the ordeal came he did not run away. And he did not even get his angels to help him.

As a man, a real man, a genuine man, he accepted his sentence, shouldered his cross and trudged weeping towards the Place of the Skull to be crucified.

I have often wondered what I should have thought had I lived in Jerusalem at the time of Jesus.

Surely my mother would have sent me with him!

Off with you, follow him, go with him to chapel, go with him to the parish church.

Listen to him, stay close to him. How good he is!

And I am sure that I should have followed him gladly.

I should certainly have gathered olive branches to throw in his path that famous day of his entry into Jerusalem.

I should have clapped my hands with faith on seeing his deeds and hearing his words.

Yes, I am sure I should.

But I am just as sure that on Good Friday things would have been different.

Meanwhile my mother would be saying to me: Boy, stay at home today. Can't you see all those people in the streets. My word, what a lot of soldiers!

Don't go out. It's dangerous. Stay indoors and watch from the window.

And I should have gone to the window like any other boy, curious to know how things would turn out.

And Jesus passed right under my window. I saw him walking in chains to Calvary.

My mother would have tried to console me: Watch carefully, Carlo. Look – you'll soon see what will happen.

Jesus is the Messiah, but he is the 'man of sorrows' too, as Isaiah called him (Isa. 53:3). You'll see, he'll go to his execution, but then – you'll see, he won't die! You'll see, he'll come down from the cross. You'll see the angels! You'll see the miracle.

As Moses crossed the Red Sea and defeated Pharaoh, so

Jesus, the new Moses, will deliver us from the executioners. He'll come down from the cross, and followed by the angels and the Zealots (they are armies – even Peter has a knife under his tunic) – he'll go into the Temple and inaugurate the messianic age we've been hoping for for so long.

Watch, young sharp-eyes. Pay close attention!

What can you see, Carlo?

I can see they've nailed him to those boards! I can see him shaking his head. I can see a soldier giving him something to drink with a sponge.

Keep on looking. Don't miss anything!

Now you'll see the miracle.

And I went on looking.

What can you see?

I see that Jesus has bowed his head.

I think I heard a shout too . . .

Mother, he's dead! Mother! He's not moving!

And my mother, like a good Jewess and knowing the synagogue catechism by heart, in the face of this collapse of our messianic faith, would have said to me: 'He has deceived us all. He was an impostor. Just another impostor. You see, it's impossible for the Messiah to die. Impossible!'

And what about me?

I should have said to myself: 'If my mother says so. . . . But how good he was!'

Could I have kept my faith under the blow of that ordeal?

I do not think so. I am no richer in faith than other people.

The novelty of the Spirit was yet to come.

The new Church was yet to be born.

The secret hidden in the ages was yet to be revealed.

No one had ever imagined that life would be born from death, and that the Messiah would have reigned from the gallows. This required something more than logic, even that of all the theologians put together.

It was a revelation. And what a revelation!

Believing that henceforth we should win by losing defied all sense. Believing that God intended to inaugurate the kingdom of love freely given, the kingdom in which the poor were to be first and the rich overthrown in their uselessness and stupidity; believing in such an inversion of values would have been beyond our wildest imagination!

The Spirit had to come.

And the Spirit did come.

And then we believed.

Really?

Have we really believed?

Seriously believed?

Goodness! How difficult it is to believe in the sort of Messiah that Jesus of Nazareth represents!

To believe that we win by losing our very selves!

To believe that love is everything.

To believe that power is a great danger, wealth slavery, comfortable life a misfortune.

It is not easy.

This is why you hear men in the street say, 'If there was a God there would not be all this suffering.'

Two thousand years have gone, and there are still Christians whose doctrinal notions belong to those ancient days when the power and existence of God was revealed by displays of strength and the victory of armies. And especially by wealth and having many possessions.

The real secret had not then been received.

Nor is it received very easily even today.

Hence the blasphemy in general circulation denying the kingdom's visibility, given the ordeal of suffering and death.

The old teaching that we, the Church, must be strong still feeds our determination to possess the land and dominate the world.

'We must make ourselves felt. We must keep our enemies down. We must scowl. We must win, and to win we need money, money, money. And to have money we need banks, we need the means and we need clever bankers. How can we do good without means, without money? Let's have a big meeting, and then any opposition will be shamed into silence. Well, we must defend our rights, the rights of the Church. We must defeat our enemies.'

Enemies, always enemies on the Church's horizon! Yet

Jesus has told us in no uncertain terms that we no longer have any enemies, since they are the same people we are supposed to love, and love specially.

Can it be that we have not understood?

Don't we read the Gospel in our churches?

How long shall we wait before following the teaching of Jesus?

When shall we learn to come into a crowd dressed as Jesus used to dress, as Francis dressed, instead of for a fashion parade, impressive and glittering like the priests in the courts of the Temple in Jerusalem?

Was nothing changed by the passage of Jesus of Nazareth?

Have we made no effort to grasp his motives for substituting humility for pride, simplicity for complication, poverty for wealth, service for power?

Should not the holy wars, the crusades, the ranks of Christians drawn up to defend the privileges of the Church, be over and done with by now?

You see, it is hard to understand and even harder to live the true privilege of those who follow Christ: the privilege of the cross.

The fact of the matter is that in my old pagan heart I have got to grasp the meaning of the Beatitudes.

They sound so unconvincing to the sort of Christians we are, who have received baptism like the squirt of a water-pistol. Let us read these Beatitudes again that offer us no blessedness whatever. Let us read them again if only to shame ourselves.

How happy are the poor in spirit;
theirs is the kingdom of heaven.
Happy the gentle:
they shall have the earth for their heritage.
Happy those who mourn:
they shall be comforted.
Happy those who hunger and thirst for what is right:
they shall be satisfied.
Happy the merciful:
they shall have mercy shown them.

Happy the pure in heart:
they shall see God.
Happy the peacemakers:
they shall be called sons of God.
Happy those who are persecuted in the cause of right:
theirs is the kingdom of heaven.

Happy are you when people abuse you and persecute you
and speak all kinds of calumny against you on my
account.
Rejoice and be glad, for your reward will be great in
heaven; this is how they persecuted the prophets before
you.   (Matt. 5:3–12)

And yet, in spite of us and our pagan heart, Jesus has
inaugurated the kingdom.
And this kingdom is coming to completion.
It is growing like a seed, growing all the time even if the
farmer does not constantly go and look at it. Isaiah says:

Yes, the heavens are as high above earth
as my ways are above your ways,
my thoughts above your thoughts.

Yes, as the rain and the snow come down from the heavens
and do not return without watering the earth, making it
yield and giving growth to provide seed for the sower and
bread for the eating,
so the word that goes from my mouth does not return to
me empty, without carrying out my will and succeeding
in what it was sent to do.   (Isa. 55:9–11)

This is the truth.
The will of God is fulfilled in spite of us . . . and even with
us sometimes.
The water of his word – says the prophet full of hope –
does not return to him without effect, 'without carrying out
my will and succeeding in what it was sent to do'.

Yes, the kingdom is fulfilled, and even if hindered it is still fulfilled.

There will still be power-seekers even in Christian clothing. But there will also be saints.

Many people will go on clinging to the old Adam's way of thinking, concentrating on righteousness and formal worship, but deep in the hearts of those visited by the Spirit of Jesus there will be an explosion, the novelty of the kingdom will erupt there and little by little, day by day, good will gain the upper hand over evil, mercy over revenge, willingness to serve over selfish prideful interest.

Above all there will be more and more of those who joyfully receive the scandalous words Jesus said to the brigand who made his confession beside him on the cross: 'today you will be with me in paradise' (Luke 23:43).

So drastic an absolution for so real a sinner may seem a bit forced.

Not to be shocked by it means you have indeed made a great leap forward in understanding mercy.

This is the leap into the kingdom of grace freely given, the kingdom which even prostitutes and publicans will enter ahead of you if you have trusted in your own presumed righteousness.

This is the kingdom of the poor, the triumph of those on the margin of society, the oppressed, the last and the least.

This is the kingdom the currency of which is forgiveness, where the banks amass only those treasures produced by human love and suffering.

This is the kingdom where the race for money and comfort does not exist, only the race for mutual service and love of your neighbour.

This is the kingdom where the highest status is martyrdom.

How extraordinary, to see all our values reversed, to see the mighty tumble from their thrones, as Mary sings in the Magnificat! Let's try to recite it with her.

My soul proclaims the greatness of the Lord
and my spirit exults in God my saviour;
because he has looked upon his lowly handmaid.

Yes, from this day forward all generations will call me
    blessed,
for the Almighty has done great things for me.
Holy is his name,
and his mercy reaches from age to age for those who fear
    him.
He has shown the power of his arm,
he has routed the proud of heart.
He has pulled down princes from their thrones and exalted
    the lowly.
The hungry he has filled with good things, the rich sent
    empty away.
He has come to the help of Israel his servant, mindful of
    his mercy
– according to the promise he made to our ancestors –
of his mercy to Abraham and to his descendants for ever.

(Luke 1:46–55)

These are the words of someone who has plumbed the
secret hidden in the ages to its depths.

7 The Price of Blood

Yes! The true secret hidden in the ages is the crucified God.

He is a God who annihilates himself for love, in Christ, and to save his creatures pays with his blood.

Whoever has painted a terrible punishing God, a damning God, should destroy that picture, fall on his knees and ask forgiveness for attributing a capacity for revenge to him.

He who has told us, 'Love your enemies, do good to those who hate you' (Luke 6:27), is scarcely likely to behave by another standard himself!

Love, real love, can only help, re-create, wait, and even say on the cross to the criminal who turns to him, 'today you will be with me in paradise'.

What hope, what sweetness there is in this terrible scene on Calvary! And the Church itself, the Church of Jesus, is born at this moment in an encounter between God and man when love achieves the miracle of eternal reconciliation.

'Today you will be with me in paradise.'

This is God's today.

This is the Church's today.

This is completely new.

This is the price of blood. Human beings are vanquished by the blood of a God.

Certainly we could never have managed to discover this true face of God had it not been for the Incarnation. And had it not been for the passion and death of Jesus.

And if we had no Gospel in our hands to tell us, criminals, delinquents and traitors that we are, this tremendous 'today, today, today you will be with me in paradise'.

It seems inconceivable that there could ever be words of absolution so drastic and so overwhelming.

And they are addressed to us who were so sure that this bandit surprised by death would end up in the eternal punishments decreed by justice!

What does he mean, this scandalous God, at the tribunal of life acquitting delinquents and pronouncing them worthy of love?

Yes, this is a scandalous God.

A God who does not hesitate to unhinge the sacred to defend the centrality of man.

Do you remember the diatribe occasioned by the disciples when they made bold to gather a few ears of corn on a day when religion forbade it, in breach of the law?

'The sabbath was made for man, not man for the sabbath' (Mark 2:27).

It is the human being that counts, not the law.

And it is for mankind that Jesus dies, demonstrating in action the value of man.

We were not accustomed to this.

We were more accustomed to liquidating those who broke the law, torturing them if they sinned, consigning them to hell if justice caught up with them.

And instead Jesus dies for them. He says the sabbath was made for them.

What dignity accrues to mankind defended by Jesus and purchased by the blood of God!

And yet we are still hung up on the law. After two thousand years of hearing this proclamation we still think it right to be tough on certain types of sinners. A short sharp shock is no bad thing!

Or perhaps it might be as well if so-and-so who might endanger the morals of the churches was kept at arm's length.

When I think how modernist priests were treated in the days of Pius X I sorrow over a Church ever tempted to turn back and so hard put to accept Jesus's way of forgiveness.

When I think of the religious wars and the strange logic of the Holy See with heretics and witches I cannot help but think how easy it is to receive baptism, and how difficult to learn to love as Christ has taught us!

How is it possible to ignore Jesus's beautiful parables on mercy, and not to realize that the actual secret about love which he revealed undercuts all religions preoccupied with defending morality and justice, and keen – as it seems – on always having someone to condemn?

The fact of the matter is that loving is difficult. And so is forgiving, truly forgiving.

It is difficult for us and hard for the Church.

Since forgiving an adulteress or an ex-priest irks the sensibilities of the 'body religious' it is easier to put that body's interests before the plain word of God. To avoid causing scandal, to set a good example, it is wiser not to accept the scandal of the cross which in any case offends our sense of justice! To defend morals it is more sensible to excommunicate someone, to deprive someone of the Eucharist.

By so doing we avoid offending a community that wants to see justice done, that feels the need to see a sinner punished.

We have not succeeded in grasping that we have been bought at the price of blood and that, as Jesus said, 'A man can have no greater love than to lay down his life for his friends' (John 15:13).

And God himself has given us the example.

Human beings are worth the price of blood.

Love is superior to law.

Forgiveness is the first law of the community willed by Jesus.

Let us not forget this.

Though we are convinced that justice and enlightened behaviour require us to uphold the law, punish the erring, refuse to overlook a person's transgression when the innocent have suffered, we must also remember there is a contrary law which systematizes things much better than we can and, as far as the thirst for restoring the balance of justice is concerned, is much more demanding and harsher than we are.

Having discovered this by personal experience I then realized that God does not renounce justice, even though he has washed me with his blood.

That law is this: human beings punish themselves by their own malice.

People who sin enter their own hell of their own volition and are constrained by the very mechanism they have themselves set in motion to drink to the dregs the bitter cup of their mistakes, their arrogance, their selfishness, their disobedience to the law of God.

No, brothers and sisters, there is no joy for the sinner, there is no future for the fugitive from love.

If you leave the Father's house where on earth can you run to? Where can you find peace, serenity, contemplation, or joy once you have rejected love?

Such audacity will be crushed under the hammer of vice. For such, anguish will haunt their nights, fear make them slaves, idolatry lead them to mortal weariness. No one can live without God: who flees him is already in hell.

When the prodigal comes home filthy, stinking, starving – would you like to see his father give him a good hiding?

The real hiding has already been administered in a life far from home – in the pit called sin, world, city, the good life.

Have you never observed the sadness deep in the eyes of someone on the run from love?

Do you not know the tortures the sinful city undergoes?

Long ago the great modern city used to frighten me – the terrible darkness where people wallow in sensuality, where violence and outrage are at home, where people laugh like lunatics and take their sport in doing one another down.

It seemed to me like the defeat of God.

There, one did the very opposite of what the Gospel taught.

There, the 'world' defined by Jesus Christ himself with his terrible judgment, 'I am not praying for the world' (John 17:9), could be truly said to be present and triumphant. This was the anti-gospel.

Now that I understand, now that I have tasted the sweetness of the Beatitudes, I can say with conviction that the world, that world, punishes itself unaided, digs its hell with its own hands, prepares its own despair with its insane will, creates its own terrifying prisons, prepares its own disintegration.

Just as human beings have the ability to build the atomic bomb to kill themselves with their own hands, so they have the ability to destroy themselves with their drugs, with their madness, with their violence, with their unlove, with their lies.

And you want God to send the whole lot to hell?

There is no need, that is hell already!

For hell is the absence of God.

When I see some churchman call down eternal punishment on sinners I feel I am watching someone who has no idea of what is going on around him, someone who has no conception of what being a sinner involves, or of the way mankind is steeped up to its neck in death.

Are you so keen on justice?

Be of good heart – justice will manage on its own without your priestly definitions.

If things are not well with this world, if there is no peace, if everyone is anxious, it is because the garden given by God in Eden has been transformed into a putrid sewer.

If there is a workman out of work, if there is a hungry baby, ask not whether God exists, ask rather what the powers that be, these miserable politicians and grafters, intend to do about it.

If the mother has cancer, if the children have leukaemia, if the forests are dying, if the sea stinks and the rivers have no fish, ask not if nature is hostile, ask what human greed has caused by destroying everything of beauty in its thirst for acquisitions.

Terrible is the hell created by human beings with their own hands!

The hospitals are full of victims, the asylums are crammed with maniacs whose vices have dissolved their brains, the gaols are the sign of a slavery that knows no bounds.

Poor us!

And when we suffer we wonder how God can exist?

We wonder how there can be a God of love?

Ask yourself rather how we can be so mad, so wicked! Ask

yourself whether you too are not partly responsible for this enormous *débâcle*!

Ask yourself where salvation may be found in this tempestuous sea of floating corpses!

Yes, experience has shown me a different view of things.

It is beyond belief what can happen in a world which does not accept God's existence, God's harmony, God's beauty, and builds with the very opposite: disorder, arrogance, money, vice, war.

I don't think this can last long. It will collapse in its own putrefaction.

Here you may learn the terrible truth about what sin has made of human beings.

Now you may stand aghast at God's severity!

It will strike you as impossible that God, preached to you as love, can keep silent at the cataclysm caused by mankind by disobeying his laws.

There are no limits to the violence of justice when it has a mind to show you that 'If Yahweh does not build the house, in vain the masons toil' (Ps. 127:1).

God is far severer than we are and will not hesitate to blow you to bits if you resist love.

He disintegrates you to the last cell.

He undoes all your dreams.

He destroys your half-hearted intentions.

He leaves nothing filthy, nothing ambiguous, nothing dark in you.

Then, to have you and make you understand, he makes you new, using the pieces of your shattered house.

He makes you humble, employing your defeats.

He restores your virginity by the offence of your lust.

He carries you into his kingdom, sending your entire load of disgusting errors flying.

He leads you into the wilderness and embraces you as you weep, reminding you that 'cut off from me you can do nothing' (John 15:5).

God is the tremendous synthesis of all opposites, in whom life and death conjoin, justice and mercy meet, light and darkness are his palace.

That is why it is difficult to understand how he loves, and how he shows his love by making you suffer is the secret hidden in the ages.

I died for you – he tells me on Calvary – now learn to die a little for me.

By dying you will learn the secret.

But you will only learn it if you die for love like me.

8   Love: Not to be Trifled With

In Psalm 137 there is something to shock you to the core.

I have known quite a lot of people who skipped this passage entirely.

Let us all read it through calmly.

It is the prayer of those in exile, of deportees far from their native land screaming in pain, and at the mere memory of their experiences hurling a curse upon their enemies: 'a blessing on him who takes and dashes your babies against the rock!' (Ps. 137:9)

Here is the psalm.

Beside the streams of Babylon
we sat and wept
at the memory of Zion,
leaving our harps
hanging on the poplars there.

For we had been asked
to sing to our captors,
to entertain those who had carried us off:
'Sing' they said
'some hymns of Zion'.

How could we sing
one of Yahweh's hymns
in a pagan country?
Jerusalem, if I forget you,
may my right hand wither!

May I never speak again,
if I forget you!
If I do not count Jerusalem
the greatest of my joys!

Yahweh, remember
what the Sons of Edom did
on the day of Jerusalem,
how they said, 'Down with her!
Raze her to the ground!'

Destructive Daughter of Babel,
a blessing on the man who treats you
as you have treated us,
a blessing on him who takes and dashes
your babies against the rock!

These hardly seem, surely, the proper sentiments for a prayer!

Can such rage be possible?

Is it possible to say in a prayer, 'a blessing on him who takes and dashes your babies against the rock'?

Is it?

Can I be persuaded that the author of this plea is the Holy Spirit – the same God who so powerfully enjoins me, 'Love your enemies, do good to those who hate you' (Luke 6:27)?

How can I believe that?

Here we are certainly faced with one of the many paradoxes of the Bible; only later in maturity do we come to grasp their significance.

On earth in our weakness we can only approach the truth through what is called a 'synthesis of opposites'.

Let us take an example.

I say: God is the cause of all things. And this is true.

Then how do I handle freedom? What then of freewill, human freewill? I then say: We each have to make our own soul.

Which is true?

Does God save us or do we save ourselves?

The truth lies in the synthesis of opposites and it is not easy to find the meeting-point.

I know that God saves me, and I know it is up to me to save myself by making an effort.

Or again:

I say that God is merciful, and this is true. God is love.

And suddenly the Word says to me, 'It is a dreadful thing to fall into the hands of the living God' (Heb. 10:31).

Where is the truth?

Is it in mercy, or in terror?

Is it in heaven, or hell?

The synthesis of opposites is plainly the way by which the word of God throughout the Bible introduces us gradually to the truth, the whole truth.

Truth proceeds by contraries.

'It's all God,' I exclaim. Then I realize that 'it's all me' too.

God is love, I sing – and then feel Jesus's sweat in Gethsemane on my own skin.

Now what kind of love is that, the love of a God who makes his Son sweat blood?

How can I possibly believe in the goodness and mercy of the Absolute if he allows me to starve to death?

Or if he makes his Son sweat blood?

This is the real problem.

As regards Psalm 137, what is the meaning of this cry for justice, this scream of those who – deported to Babylon after seeing their own children smashed against the walls of Jerusalem – defiantly shout at the enemy, 'a blessing on him who takes and dashes your babies against the rock'?

This is not the cry of God seeking revenge but the plaint of a human being seeking to understand.

'Beware, mankind, beware!

'I saw how you smashed the deportees' babies against the ramparts of Jerusalem.

'And I have taken their side.'

God is on the side of the poor, the exile, the deportee.

Mankind, remember that!

Yes, there is Someone in the world watching, noting, recording, remembering.

Nor does this Someone let matters take their course, or let you think that good and evil are the same thing, or with impunity spill the blood of others as casually as you might pour yourself a drink.

You would like to forget. He cannot forget.

And why not?

Because love is God's substance, and it must become your substance if you wish to become his child.

And how can it become your substance if you fail to understand?

By having the guts to go through the same sort of suffering as you have inflicted on others?

Yes. To understand you have to go through it yourself. That is the only way you will ever learn, blockhead!

Go through it yourself. See what it feels like.

The children of Babylon did not realize how wicked it was when they smashed the skulls of the children of Jerusalem against their city walls. They will understand better when they know how it feels to see their own babies smashed on the rocks.

This time the babies are theirs. Now they will have a standard of comparison for what they have done to other people's babies.

This is terrible!

Our inability to get to the truth except by bitter experience is terrible!

Sisters and brothers: I tremble at what I am about to tell you. But I am going to say it all the same because I am convinced it is true.

I now know why there is so much suffering and weeping in the world.

It was not God who sent it. It was ourselves who willed it, we who chose it!

It was we rich nations sucking the blood of poor nations who established the spiral of violence, hatred and war. We who, betraying a girl's love, disrupted her life and thrust her into the insecurity of prostitution.

It was our selfishness that brought whole species to extinction, our pride that caused the weeping that surrounds us. At this point isn't it natural that he who is the world's memory, he who keeps the record of our flight towards the void, should decide to block our way?

And obviously our way cannot be blocked with words.

So many have been addressed to us already and we have not listened!

The way to block our way is by suffering, and he knows how to employ it.

Once we have been betrayed by someone we begin to appreciate our own betrayals. Once we experience for ourselves hunger, plague, war, we get some idea of the wickedness and cruelty with which we have treated others. Once we are deserted we recall that we too have deserted someone else.

If we have ever behaved abruptly to an invalid, once we are ill ourselves we behave more calmly, more sympathetically.

Suffering in our own flesh is the only way of learning to love anyone else properly.

In times of trial lust becomes friendship, friendship becomes sharing, sharing becomes agape.

God touches us in our flesh because the tears issuing from that flesh teach us how to mature in the things of God.

What would become of us if it were not for suffering?

We should plunge to disintegration, to the nothingness that theologians call hell.

I do not waste time wondering about the existence of hell.

It is a useless question, if you read the Gospel aright.

Instead, the point is not to go there and to find someone to block my way before it is too late.

That is what happened to the prodigal son in Luke's Gospel.

The fugitive was blocked by hunger. He came home because he was hungry.

It is not very elegant, not very romantic, but that's the way things are.

And God does not fret too much over details.

For him the important thing was to save his child, and he did it by means of hunger.

Sometimes he uses things that hurt even more than that.

God's love is terrible when he has a mind to save us!

It crushes us to pieces, smashes us, rather than lose us.

And not losing us means that we for our part come to understand.

It means understanding that love is not to be trifled with.

Understanding means entering into the sufferings of our sisters and brothers.

It means understanding that our pride causes wounds around us, that our greed is starving someone, that our lust is making use of someone else and depriving that person of freedom.

All too readily we say: Why the suffering of the world, why the pain of the innocent, why hunger, why war?

We should do better to say: We rich nations have sucked the blood of the poor, and now we wonder why there are starving babies in Brazil.

You, mighty nation bent on extending your influence, sell guns and tanks to poor nations and then say: Poor nations have no idea how to live and let live.

What would the world be like if the mighty and the weak began respecting one another, began respecting human beings, and above all began helping one another? What would happen if we became, or tried to become, brothers?

Earth would be a paradise; suffering would be immeasurably reduced.

I am certain that the mighty mountain of universal suffering afflicting us on earth is due first and foremost to human sin, to our violence, pride, lust, selfishness and greed.

Let me be plain: the immense catastrophes of war, social struggle, tribal clashes, famine, ecological imbalance, and so on are due to our disobeying the clear and simple laws of God, nature and life.

And that is no small thing.

One point remains to be cleared up, something that haunts me about suffering.

What about the innocent? What about the victims of the arrogance of the arrogant?

What about those who endure the wickedness of others?

What about the babies?

9 The Primacy of Martyrdom

If the secret hidden in the ages is that of a crucified God, who with his love breaks the chain of violence and outrage to inaugurate the age of reconciliation and peace, then the most beautiful photograph of him is the one taken by Isaiah, seven centuries before Christ, with the flashlamp of his prophetic spirit, in all the detail recorded for us in the fourth song of the servant of Yahweh:

Like a sapling he grew up in front of us,
like a root in arid ground.
Without beauty, without majesty (we saw him),
no looks to attract our eyes;
a thing despised and rejected by men,
a man of sorrows and familiar with suffering,
a man to make people screen their faces;
he was despised and we took no account of him.

And yet ours were the sufferings he bore,
ours the sorrows he carried.
But we, we thought of him as someone punished,
struck by God, and brought low.
Yet he was pierced through for our faults,
crushed for our sins.
On him lies a punishment that brings us peace,
and through his wounds we are healed.

We had all gone astray like sheep,
each taking his own way,
and Yahweh burdened him

with the sins of all of us.
Harshly dealt with, he bore it humbly,
he never opened his mouth,
like a lamb that is led to the slaughter-house,
like a sheep that is dumb before its shearers
never opening its mouth.

By force and by law he was taken;
would anyone plead his cause?
Yes, he was torn away from the land of the living;
for our faults struck down in death.
They gave him a grave with the wicked,
a tomb with the rich,
though he had done no wrong
and there had been no perjury in his mouth.
Yahweh has been pleased to crush him with suffering.

(Isa. 53:2–10)

Nor is Isaiah content with photographing the mystery of the Just One, the image of the suffering servant, the poor man of Yahweh, but makes it clear that by this means he won the victory.

Christ does not die to lose the battle with evil. He dies to vanquish evil, he dies to 'see his heirs'. What millions of them there have been!

He dies to 'have a long life' (Isa. 53:10).

With the revelation of Jesus crucified is born the Church, the society of those who believe in him, who re-created by his Spirit have become capable of carrying out God's intent to overcome evil with good.

Thus martyrdom is born with its indisputable primacy.

Henceforth what counts for spreading the kingdom is not power but service, not revenge but forgiveness, not pride but humility, not culture but blood.

The primacy of martyrdom is an absolute not only for Jesus but for each one of us.

We must get this fact firmly into our heads, for now all the perspectives are different and love's imperative is now our imperative.

It won't do any more to say: One has paid the price for all. That is too easy.

Calculating business-people like ourselves cannot go on foisting the whole weight of our wickedness on to the blood of Jesus.

For sensual people like us it is all too convenient a solution to the problem of the 'good life' lived to the last degree of idolatry, to reassure ourselves by saying that, on the cross, someone else has paid for our insanity.

No! That won't do any more!

We must fill up in ourselves, as Paul says, 'all that has still to be undergone by Christ' (Col. 1:24).

Love will make demands on us. It will question us from within. It will disturb us. Sadden us. Play havoc with our feelings. Harass us. Reveal our superficialities. But at last it will bring us to the light.

The light that flashes forth from love is the thirst for martyrdom.

Jesus instituted true martyrdom, and his friends and followers will love martyrdom too.

The primacy of martyrdom will be the apex of their scale of values.

Martyrdom begins by telling you: 'Today your martyrdom will be to detach yourself from your wealth. You will have to be detached if you want to be happy, for wealth will destroy your peace of mind, especially when you see your fellow-man going hungry.'

Tomorrow it will tell you: 'Don't be an idolater. Cast away your idols! God alone is your God.' And you will have to do this to slake the thirst for freedom that love has given you.

Thenceforth this process of purification will be endless, working its way down deeper and deeper to reach the roots of your selfishness, pride and folly.

And then, as you begin to remember all the terrible things you have done and the way you have made other people suffer, you will begin to feel a need to make amends.

In my mature years it has been the greatest help to me to recite the prayer attributed to St Francis:

> Lord Jesus, two graces I ask of you before I die: first, to feel in soul and body, as far as is possible, the pain that you, sweet Jesus, bore in the hour of your most bitter passion; second, to feel in my heart, as far as is possible, that extraordinary love with which you, Son of God, were so inflamed as willingly to endure so great a passion for us sinners.

What an extraordinary prayer.

I keep reciting it, even though I cannot live it, but I feel it is the true way to happiness, to self-surrender, to freedom from fear of suffering in a world that will have become the kingdom.

Yes, I am sure of it!

Only by dying of love shall I succeed in freeing myself from myself, from my idolatries, my complexes, my chains.

To die of love is the way to that happiness which is freedom, self-giving, peace, joy, eternity.

Now, do you really want to know why the innocent suffer?

Does it shock you that some people in this world pay the price, bedridden or stuck in a wheelchair?

Do you wonder why suffering should be our common universal lot?

Does it really shock you to have to suffer a bit?

Rather, dear brothers and sisters, you should be wondering how we can bear to live in selfishness and arrogance.

Wonder and tremble: How can it come about that one Central American family should own a whole province, treating the farmers there as slaves, when the poor do not even have a handful of beans to feed their children?

Ask yourself, appalled: How is it possible for dictators to torture anyone trying to throw off the fetters of pharaonic power?

That's what you ought to be wondering about.

The child who dies in a state of innocence is actually the

lucky one – the one who pays the price for the unjust and the wicked; he is on the same road as Jesus. He who gives his blood for children heads the great procession of mankind towards the heavenly Jerusalem.

Blessed are you, innocents of Bethlehem slaughtered by the cruelty of Herod.

How lucky you are who not with words but with blood have borne witness to the coming of Christ on earth. Blessed are you, martyrs of all the ages, who have chosen true love and given your blood for its sake.

Blessed are you, massacred army of saints who have celebrated your mass as priests of Christ the eternal priest.

Blessed are you, the poor of all the ages.

Blessed are you, men and women of peace.

Blessed are you the pure of heart.

Blessed are you who thirst for justice.

Blessed are you the persecuted.

Blessed are you who have turned the other cheek.

Blessed are you the non-violent.

Blessed are you, Francis.

Blessed are you, Gandhi.

Blessed are you, Romero.

Blessed are you, Popieluszko.

Blessed are you unsung martyrs of all totalitarian regimes of East and West.

Blessed are you, imprisoned innocent trampled under the iron boot of power.

Blessed are you, child of the third world with your belly distended with hunger.

Blessed are you, poor mother, grubbing through the refuse of the rich to feed your children.

Blessed, blessed!

And why? Why blessed?

Because by your presence and your martyrdom you scream the path of salvation and love to us.

You preach the Gospel.

Is there a school in the world more true than yours?

Is there a cry in the universe more shattering than yours?

At sight of you, love is unleashed in those touched by the

Spirit. At the sound of your scream the good set out for the goal.

Your existence reveals the injustice of the world, your sufferings are the fuel of our universal purgatory.

Could we have Francis without the leper?

We call Francis blessed as he kisses the leper. And we are right to do so. But I say to the leper: You are more blessed than he.

The true blessedness of the last day is the blessedness of the lowest place, the place whence rises to God the cry for rescue from human injustice and sin.

And God feels this so strongly that he has unhesitatingly taken the last place himself.

Father de Foucauld says: 'Jesus took the lowest place in such a way that no one has ever been able to take it from him.'

That is the right place for Love.

No, do not wonder why the innocent suffer.

Do not be puzzled at seeing a handicapped person in a wheelchair, or a blind man crossing the street with his dog.

Get used to saying whenever you see the handicapped or the blind crossing your path: Blessed are you, blessed are you!

And get out of the habit of saying this when you see the mighty: him, lolling in opulence and wealth; her, dolled up in fatuity.

Luke the evangelist tells you what to say to them!

'Alas for you . . . alas for you . . . alas for you . . .' (Luke 6:24-6).

As you see, brothers and sisters, it is not easy to take the side of the Gospel!

But it means being on the side of truth, courage and love.

There is nothing terrible about suffering a bit on earth if it has taught you how to love.

The terrible thing is the quest for selfish pleasure, leading to revulsion and death.

It is no great matter to undergo a time of distress if it wins you the safety of your children.

The pity is to be indifferent to your mother's tears.

Brothers and sisters, if there is a kingdom, and if that kingdom is eternal, Francis was right to say:

So great the good I have in sight,
That every pain is my delight.

10 'He Struck Jacob's Hip in the Socket'

At the beginning of the long history of the people of God stands the towering figure of Jacob.

Son of Isaac, grandson of Abraham the great forbear of believers, Jacob is a mature accomplished, cunning individual.

He is the kind to fight all comers, even God. Which is exactly what happened at the ford of the Jabbok.

We are even told that when in his mother's womb he fought so furiously with his twin brother Esau that when Esau managed to emerge from the waters first, thus becoming the firstborn, Jacob was holding him by the heel, as if to say, 'You've robbed me of my inheritance! But I'll have it back from you, the first chance I get!'

And he did, taking advantage of Esau's gluttony and hunger with a nice plate of lentils he had cooked for him.

But the matter was not as simple as all that and became such a bone of contention between them that the brothers ran a serious risk of harming each other, since they were incapable of seeing eye to eye.

Jacob was afraid of his brother's strength. Esau was a bit on the tough side. And Jacob was always trying to get the better of him by cunning and gifts.

He succeeded. And we find him in the fullness of his manhood no longer fighting his brother, but God.

The story of Jacob's struggle with God is fantastic, there at the ford of the Jabbok separating him from the land he was destined to conquer, symbolising power and wealth.

Jacob is at the peak of his powers.

He is rich and capable; he has chariots, camels, fertile wives and innumerable children.

One night . . .

Yes, one night he had a presentiment that something extraordinary was about to happen, something that would mark him forever.

He told nobody about this.

He wanted to be alone.

Scripture says:

That same night he rose, and taking his two wives and his two slave-girls and his eleven children he crossed the ford of the Jabbok.

He took them and sent them across the stream and sent all his possessions over too.

And Jacob was left alone.   (Gen. 32:23–5)

Then comes the mysterious sentence: 'And there was one that wrestled with him until daybreak' (Gen. 32:26).

At the ford Jacob wrestled with an angel, a manifestation and sign of God himself.

This struggle between man and God holds a place in mystical history for all time, and many an artist has risked his reputation trying to represent what must have happened on the smooth rocks of that stream-bed.

What happened to Jacob there in the heat of battle, holding fast to the angel who kept thrusting him away but seemed somehow to love him?

This is the eternal struggle on earth between man and God.

This is their effort to come to an understanding, to a common will for salvation in the infinite complications of history.

I do not know what may have happened to you in that torrent. I only know what happened to me.

I too have fought. I too have had to struggle between my will and God's will, between his way of doing things and mine.

I truly believe the story of Jacob is everybody's story.

The story of man striving with God on the highway of existence.

It is man's dramatic prayer.

The question forever posed by our experience.

It is the experience of living on earth as in a dark night.

The locus of the contingent being us against the Absolute of God.

The school of a freedom painfully won, to become God's children in the truest sense and discard the remaining fetters of our slavery.

One day Jesus will say: 'I shall not call you servants any more . . . I call you friends' (John 15:15; cf Mark 14:36; Matt. 26:42).

And a friend knows what a friend wants.

But we struggle as though viable, more human, more normal, more humanly acceptable alternatives existed.

Even Jesus strove with his Father during that tremendous night in Gethsemane.

And came out of it with blood oozing from his pores and dripping on the ground, as Luke records.

'. . . let your will be done, not mine,' Jesus will say (Luke 22:43), but only at the end of the struggle.

There are different wills, then, if even Jesus says so.

What could Jesus's will have been in contrast to the will of the Father?

Certainly not an evil will.

Like us in every way except sin (Heb. 4:15), Jesus striving in Gethsemane could not have desired a messianic fulfilment of any sort other than good.

If we may be allowed to consider for a moment what Jesus in the extremity of his ordeal could have desired by way of fulfilment of his messianic dream, surely it had to do with the good of mankind.

'Father! Is it really necessary for me to die in this fashion?

'When people see that I have been crucified, will that make it easier for them to understand that you are a father?

'Wouldn't it be better if I, as Messiah, were to take power in Jerusalem and impose the well-being of mankind by force of law?

'Wouldn't it be better if I used religious power to promote a policy of equality and prosperity?

'Wouldn't it be better to give people the food they want, the housing they need, the political freedom to which they aspire in their struggle with the Romans?'

If Jesus did have some alternative in mind it must have been about the way the Messiah was to achieve justice on earth.

There were two alternatives: power or service – law or love – dying on the cross or crucifying the enemy.

It is not always feasible to establish a synthesis of extremes.

There are times when one extreme must have primacy over the other.

The Father asked Jesus for the primacy of love.

It would be difficult to grasp at first!

But eventually mankind would get the point.

Anyhow, eternally speaking, there was no other way.

The primacy was: the primacy of martyrdom.

To return to Jacob grappling on the gravel of the torrent.

'. . . seeing that he could not master him, struck him in the socket of his hip, and Jacob's hip was dislocated as he wrestled with him' (Gen. 32:26).

Of all the symbols of this parable, this detail is the most puzzling.

To convince Jacob God wounds him – dislocates his hip, cripples him – and then calmly proceeds:

'Now you have come to know your weakness.

'Now rely on God.

'Now you will be victorious.'

And to make him realize that everything has been changed by this new tactic, he changes his name too:

'Your name shall no longer be Jacob, but Israel' (Gen. 32:29).

Israel the new man, the man crippled in the struggle with God but now able to understand the meaning of history; the man made humble by suffering, the man of sharing, the man who understands his fellow-man, the man who prays for God's help; the man who relies on God's power and not his own, the man who conquers but not in the old arrogant sensual way: the man of the Beatitudes.

Bewildered as we all are about why suffering should exist, I have often wondered whether it would not have been better to have a world without suffering, without cripples, without tears, without handicapped people, without bloodshed, without wheelchairs.

The answer has become clearer with the passing of the years.

No! Without suffering, without tears, without death, the world would be all the uglier. Worse still, mankind would be wickeder, you might even say diabolical.

If people are so wicked as it is under the heavy hand of the Crippler – without the crippling they would be unbearable!

God had infinite ways of making a different world.

He is God. He is the God of the impossible.

He could have made a world without suffering. He could have made a world not subject to pain, he could have immersed his children in the joys of *eros* as though on an endless honeymoon. But no! He has not done so.

He has allowed us a bit of *eros*. But he has asked us to get used to the agape of sacrifice.

He has given us stupendous dawns but has mingled them with tragic nights.

He has given us health and strength and has let us have holes in our lungs or cells run mad and designed to suffocate us when we least expect it. Evil can assume horrendous forms.

It is no good saying that God does not will the evil; that human guilt and an ecology in shambles are to blame for our sufferings.

That won't wash!

After all, God can do anything, and if he wished he could stop the cancer that's eating me away.

He doesn't.

I like Jacob's solution. It seems simpler to me.

It's God himself who has crippled me.

You can go on arguing forever, like the four theologians at Job's side, about why we suffer and why God permits suffering on earth.

I prefer to say: He causes it.

He destroys my fields. He lets the enemy kill my children. He has placed me on this dunghill.

There are not two forces in the universe.

There is only one: God!

He can intervene.

But he does not, and he allows me to suffer. He permits war to be declared. He says nothing when four mafia bosses corrupt the province where I live, he lets the cruel hand of the military or police torture my fellow men to 'make them talk'.

This is one part of the mystery of suffering:

God permits it.

God wounds me.

God destroys my harvests.

God rages in the storm.

God leads me to my death.

But precisely in wounding me he draws out the best in me.

If I were not wounded – how unbearable I should be in my fiendish security! How sure of myself!

Wounded, I remain calm and learn to weep. Weeping I learn to understand others, I learn the blessedness of poverty.

This is a fact.

If human beings had no pain, were never pushed to the limits of endurance, how hard it would be for them to enter the road to salvation!

If the Israelites had enjoyed freedom in Egypt, Moses could never have persuaded them to attempt the march of liberation.

If the desert had been full of beguiling oases instead of snakes, hunger and thirst, they would never have reached the Promised Land.

No spur can move us towards tomorrow more effectively than suffering.

That's why God struck Jacob on the hip.

I was in a train, praying over a text of Ezekiel.

Sitting opposite was a woman in the black shawl of a southern peasant. I noticed she was taking an interest in me.

She kept staring at my Bible, obviously intrigued.

Guessing that she had something to say, I broke the silence. I found a kindred spirit. She learned that I had been praying. She too, of course, was accustomed to pray.

And she told me her story.

'I'm from Calabria. My family and I lived in an awfully poor village.

'I was poor too.

'One day my son said, "Mother, I'm going to Milan to look for a job."

' "Very well," I said, and he left. He found work easily and settled in Milan.

'After a bit he wrote to his father, my husband. "Father, you come too! You're a bricklayer. You'll find work as well."

'So my husband went.

'In less than a year he wrote to both of my daughters: "Why don't you come too? We'll be a family again!"

'So my daughters went.

' "What am I supposed to do here on my own? I'm coming too," I wrote.

' "I'll cook your meals and keep the house in order."

'And that's what we did. I left too, and we all became Milanese.

'Now . . .'

Here the woman broke down and wept.

She wiped her tears but the sobs kept coming.

'Now we are so sad! I'd never seen so much money in my house! Four salaries!

'We are so sad.

'We have grown rich, and we have been destroyed.

'My husband is no longer the same person.

'My two daughters – why, I daren't say a word to them, even if they come home at three o'clock in the morning.

'My son? I fear for him. The company he keeps has ruined his character.

'Yes, we are so sad. We don't like one another any more! We're always angry and anxious.

'We don't sing any more!

'Back in the village we were poor, but we were happy and contented.

'When feast days came we knew how to have a good time.

'Now every day's a feast day, and we don't know how to be happy any more.

'Money has done us no good.

'Damned money!

'Things were so much better before!'

This testimony is the genuine gospel preached by a poor woman who sees things as they really are.

It seems strange and hard to understand, but this is the case:

We are afraid of being poor but we need to be poor.

We are afraid to suffer but we need to suffer – to preserve the balance of existence and to find, in pain, a corrective for sensuality and indifference.

I can testify to this from my own experience. I have seen two generations come and go.

Two generations ago people were happier. They were more serene. And they were poorer than we are. They had a much rougher life than we do.

Poverty keeps people in moral equilibrium, keeps hard-working families virtuous, sets limits to their desire for possessions, preserves humility in personal relationships, encourages them to be industrious, nourishes hope.

I say 'poverty', not misery.

Poverty is the happy medium between two curses.

The one is wealth, which is nearly always the fruit of exploitation, injustice or extortion; the other, misery, is evidence of an evil deed committed by you or by others against you.

Someone poor has a better chance of becoming a mature personality as regards matters human and divine. By nature his living is closer to that of Jesus of Nazareth, the man-God.

While living on earth he chose neither the wealth of influential Jerusalem families nor the dramatic poverty of the Baptist.

He wanted to give us an example of something easier and

more agreeable to human nature: the hard-working poverty of those who live their span on earth strenuously, cheerfully, frugally and serenely.

I am convinced that in this balance between the tensions of history and the joys of life, the struggle to earn our bread and the satisfaction of sitting down at table, the strain of living in common and the rapture of being together, we have the best means afforded us by God for fulfilling ourselves and passing our span on earth in the easiest and most fertile way.

It is not a coincidence that the Son of God in coming among us embraced a mode of life that is still, for everyone, the most natural and surest way of journeying to eternity.

Nazareth shows us how.

11 Love More to Suffer Less

If it is true that the secret hidden in the ages is the love taught us by a crucified God, then we can readily accept John's definition in his First Letter to the churches: 'God is love' (1 John 4:8).

And we might also learn by heart Paul's unforgettable page on charity, which as you know is the truest sort of love, taught us by Christ himself.

If I have all the eloquence of men or angels, but speak without love, I am simply a gong booming or a cymbal clashing. If I have the gift of prophecy, understanding all the mysteries there are, and knowing everything, and if I have faith in all its fullness, to move mountains, but without love, then I am nothing at all. If I give away all that I possess, piece by piece, and if I even let them take my body to burn it, but am without love, it will do me no good whatever.

Love is always patient and kind; it is never jealous; love is never boastful or conceited; it is never rude or selfish; it does not take offence, and is not resentful. Love takes no pleasure in other people's sins but delights in the truth; it is always ready to excuse, to trust, to hope, and to endure whatever comes.

Love does not come to an end. But if there are gifts of prophecy, the time will come when they must fail; or the gift of languages, it will not continue for ever; and knowledge – for this, too, the time will come when it must fail. For our knowledge is imperfect and our prophesying is imperfect; but once perfection comes, all imperfect things will disappear. When I was a child, I used to talk like a child, and think like a child, and argue like a child, but now I am a man, all childish ways are put behind me. Now we are seeing a dim reflection in a mirror; but then we shall be seeing face to face. The knowledge that I have now is imperfect; but then I shall know as fully as I am known.

In short, there are three things that last: faith, hope and love; and the greatest of these is love.　　(1 Cor. 13:1–13)

Love explains why God has created the world.

Love requires the Incarnation. Love speaks to you of the kingdom.

Love is the optimism of the universe, the joy of living, the impetus that thrusts you forward.

Love brings you to birth, picks you up if you fall, corrects you if you err, waits for you if you run away, enfolds you if you pause to look for it, kisses you if you kiss it.

It also makes you suffer.

This making you suffer takes us a long time to understand. Most of us look on suffering as punishment for sin. And since, as far as sin is concerned, we all commit it without stint, in our immaturity we say, 'God has punished me.'

And so we go from one 'punishment' to the next, and from one suffering to another.

But that is not the way it is.

God punishes no one, and now that I have come to know him a little I am ashamed of a time when I immaturely thought of pain as God's punishment. When all is said and done – if we think of God as a punishing God the only thing we are doing is thinking of God as being . . . like us: bad, bad, bad!

Isn't it bad to punish someone? Is punishment anything but a little vendetta?

You did not listen to me so I am punishing you!

Great stuff!

Since Jesus himself told us to turn the other cheek when someone strikes us, is he likely to act differently, and instead of the other cheek offer us a well-deserved punishment?

I shouldn't care for a God of this kind. I should try to steer clear of him rather than have him endlessly laying into me.

Having told us to turn the other cheek, for his part he has offered us his whole self to beat up, not merely his cheek.

This is certain. And yet he has not removed our suffering, even though he has forgiven us.

That would make no sense. He would be training us up in a world where good and evil were the same thing.

Which they are not.

Hence he makes us suffer.

As he sees it, the suffering he offers – and offers so liberally – is not punishment.

It is school. And it is the school of love.

This is difficult to accept, for our superficiality and selfishness are boundless.

God being love can give only love, and suffering helps us enter into love.

In this God shows how imaginative he is, by contriving to change the brute fact of punishment into a real 'growing up to love' on our part!

If he did not make us suffer we would blunder through life without understanding anything.

We should not grasp the value of things. Poetry would have no meaning and history would be deprived of its fascination and dramatic power.

How should we understand rest without weariness, joy without weeping, light without darkness, forgiveness without hatred, truth without error?

God touches us in our flesh to make us feel the needs of the world.

Your flesh becomes the book of God's language, the alphabet of the way he expresses himself.

He punishes you to make you like himself: able to love.

He takes your health away to make you small and humble, he gives darkness to make you call for light, he makes you lonely to make you look for him, he touches you in your flesh to make you feel the flesh of the world.

And he is not above making you cry. For he knows the value of tears.

And even if you suppose mere chance is what is making you suffer, rather than his specific will, he lets you cry and says nothing.

He waits for you to understand.

To understand the nexus between love and pain, death and resurrection is very hard for us – all but impossible without the Spirit.

You keep thinking that things should not be like this; they can't be!

You think you fell ill by accident; or, the reason why you fell downstairs was because it was dark that evening.

But this is not the case.

If God is God, not a drop of blood is without meaning, not one cell is out of place, no tear falls from the eye without leaving it the purer and clearer.

I should like to teach you a little trick: just the thing for someone afraid of suffering – or better still for someone trying to suffer less.

The trick is this: LOVE MORE TO SUFFER LESS.

I have tried this many a time! And although I am still taking my first steps, I can see that it works.

And I intend to get it perfect, this trick of mine, because suffering always takes us by surprise and we feel a great need of a little respite when the ordeal overtakes us!

Now that I am old I have plenty of opportunity for doing this.

Listen.

The Germans, and even more the Austrians, have a great love of candles – beautiful brightly coloured candles with different kinds of symbols and lettering on them. They make absolute masterpieces for putting on the table on a holiday, or on the altar as a sign of joy and communion.

You know the meaning of candles in church – what they symbolize.

They originate from the Passover night, the Pasch of the Lord.

The first Christians used the candle to symbolize Christ's presence in the darkness of the world.

As Christ is the light of the world and was consumed by love, so also this candle gives light by burning itself away.

It is a sign, and like all signs it has a message for us.

It has said much to me. I have watched it gleaming afar on Holy Saturday night. I have made it mine when celebrating Easter Sunday mass in community, beginning with the short ceremony of the light.

But I have gone a little further in understanding about the light that consumes the wax.

And when a dear friend of mine in Vienna presented me with one of these coloured candles I took it home to my cell and put it on my chest of drawers next to a little icon.

And now I have something like a little altar.

And now I should like to explain the trick I use.

When sorrows come upon me, as happens fairly often, and I feel as though I am down a dark hole, I light the candle. Gazing at it I try to repeat the words I find so easy to say during our public ceremony of the light of Christ.

'Do you see this candle? It is the symbol of Jesus who gives light to the world by being consumed, as this candle is consumed.'

Now let me say right from the start that to say this to others is easier than saying it to yourself. But I say it and try to take courage.

And then what do I do?

Continuing my little personal liturgy, I do three things.

Little things that have occurred to me, leading in the right direction.

I pray.

I love.

I wait.

As for praying, this is not the moment to come out with some magnificent speech to God.

I just say a prayer appropriate to a poor man like myself, and every time I say it I like it better because it is simple and says it all in a few words.

When I feel like that I love this prayer. I say it once for every bead of the rosary I am holding. Here it is! 'Help comes to me from Yahweh, who made heaven and earth' (Ps. 121:2).

Then I remind myself: calling for help is not enough, praying is not enough. As Jesus has told us, it is not those who keep saying, 'Lord, Lord', who will enter the kingdom of heaven (Matt. 7:21; cf. Luke 6:46).

That is too easy. One must do more.

And doing more brings us back to the same theme I have been repeating over and over throughout this book, at the risk of boring you:

Love, Carlo.

Make an effort in the right direction: in the direction of Christ the lover.

I rarely feel that I have no reason to love.

I have long known that if I want to be happy on earth I must fall madly in love with God and the things of God.

Then, all things being equal, in time of suffering the easiest way to allay the suffering, especially if it is really sharp, is to get out of myself – yes, get out of myself, visit someone who is suffering worse than I am, do something to remind me of the sufferings of the world, set my heart in order if I feel a residual dislike of someone, write a cheque for the world's poorest mission, answer a tiresome letter from someone who wants me to tell him whether hell exists, or what he should not do to leave his nasty possessive wife.

In other words, perform an act of love that requires patience and honesty.

If I were younger I should willingly go out and spend an hour playing cards with an old age pensioner living alone and dying of loneliness. I should take the opportunity of emptying his chamber-pot and dabbing a drop of scent on his sheets.

That done, what else is to be done as the candle goes on burning itself away?

One very simple thing. But something very real and necessary.

Wait.

And while I am waiting that passage from Scripture always comes to mind: 'It is good to wait in silence for Yahweh to save' (Lam. 3:26).

Then I usually fall asleep, so I don't know what happens next.

But at last I feel better.

Brothers and – even more – sisters, if perchance you try this liturgy, think of my candle and I shall think of yours!

Let us help one another, for suffering is always hard to bear and helping our neighbour is a virtuous deed.

For my part I have found no other help but prayer. And I see from reading the Gospel that Jesus did the same thing. Luke, who was a physician and knew what he was talking about, says that when Jesus was in Gethsemane in the tremendous exertion of suffering, entering his agony: '*prolixius orabat*'. What fine Latin: '. . . *factus in agonia, prolixius orabat*'. And that fine sounding Latin means in simple words: 'In his anguish he prayed even more earnestly' (Luke 22:44).

To lessen his pain, which was atrocious, he prayed all the more, he spoke even harder to the Father. Yes, he prayed more, as if by praying more he could lessen his pain and make it endurable.

Remember this, brothers and sisters. I dare say my little trick will help you.

Of course, you may laugh at me instead. What a simple fellow! How childish!

When you get old you reach your second childhood. I like childish things.

Besides, I may as well tell you – when I do these things I always feel close to my mother who died years ago, but whom I expect to see again soon.

I am so close to her.

No one speaks to me as she does.

But if you like grown-up things and grown-up talk, I can talk like that too, I'm not afraid; but I shall tell you straight away: none of you would put what I say into practice.

The kingdom of heaven is not made for grown-ups.

Listen.

There is a trick for grown-ups too, very much like mine: *Love more and you will suffer less.*

But who has the courage to do it?

Even India, poor as she is, has decided to build an atomic bomb. For shame! What about her great patriarch Gandhi?

No, it is not easy to grasp that the only way to suffer less is to love more, especially in politics. At the risk of seeming weaker. Yes, at the risk of seeming weaker I shall not build an atomic bomb, I shall not give my enemy a whack in the eye to show that I am stronger, I shall not make war, I shall not squash my tomatoes and apples with a tractor to keep the price up, I shall not destroy forests to build factories, I shall not poison the sea.

If love is the rule of my politics and the thrust of my action, yes, I really shall suffer less and I shall cause less suffering in others, some I shall be loving more.

It is much harder being great. And – a real obstacle to entering the kingdom.

12   Pray More to Suffer Less

*A short guide for three days of prayer
after the example of three great women
Marianella García Villas
Benedetta Bianchi Porro
Veronica Giuliani*

I thought I would end this book about suffering by inviting the reader to pray.

It is never a mistake to pray and I am convinced that the power of prayer is irresistible.

The prayers are here arranged in the form of brief offices for private or communal use, corresponding to Lauds in the morning or Vespers in the evening.

I have chosen three basic themes, one for each day, to pledge us to the school of suffering and to help us avoid the risk of reducing our piety to private, ineffectual pietism. Here are the themes.

1.   The Courage of Faith
2.   Hope in Sickness
3.   The Folly of the Cross

For each theme the instruction is developed in line with the witness of three exceptional women. Call me a feminist if you will. I firmly believe women to be more courageous in suffering than men. Be that as it may, these three special people can help us.

Marianella speaks to us about courageous faith;

Benedetta about patience in suffering;

Veronica will introduce us to the folly of the cross.

Truth to tell, all three of them are mad. God grant they may transmit to us a bit of their madness!

How fine it would be if we learned to smile at life a little and stopped complaining with every step we take!

First day

Those who trust in Yahweh are like Mount Zion . . .

(Ps. 125:1)

Prayer from the Depths of Agony

Yahweh my God, I call for help all day,
I weep to you all night;
may my prayer reach you
hear my cries for help;

for my soul is all troubled,
my life is on the brink of Sheol;
I am numbered among those who go down to the Pit,
a man bereft of strength:

a man alone, down among the dead,
among the slaughtered in their graves,
among those you have forgotten,
those deprived of your protecting hand.

You have plunged me to the bottom of the Pit,
to its darkest, deepest place,
weighted down by your anger,
drowned beneath your waves.

You have turned my friends against me
and made me repulsive to them;
in prison and unable to escape,
my eyes are worn out with suffering.

Yahweh, I invoke you all day,
I stretch out my hands to you:
are your marvels meant for the dead,
can ghosts rise up to praise you?

Who talks of your love in the grave,
of your faithfulness in the place of perdition?
Do they hear about your marvels in the dark,
about your righteousness in the land of oblivion?

But I am here, calling for your help,
praying to you every morning:
why do you reject me?
Why do you hide your face from me?

Wretched, slowly dying since my youth,
I bore your terrors – now I am exhausted;
your anger overwhelmed me,
you destroyed me with your terrors
which, like a flood, were round me, all day long,
all together closing in on me.
You have turned my friends and neighbours against me,
now darkness is my one companion left.   (Ps. 88)

2 CORINTHIANS 4:7–18

MATTHEW 18:1–10

Marianella

The Courage of Faith

Marianella García Villas, a young woman of El Salvador
killed by government troops, 13 March 1983.

Lawyer of the poor, sister to the oppressed, voice of the
vanished, Marianella's life and sacrifice are entered in the
'book of exemplars' and on the roll of Latin-American
witnesses and martyrs.

From the years of her education in a rich Spanish religious
school for girls to her identification with the poor of her
country, especially the peasants; from her activism with the
Christian Democrats to her election to the Legislative
Assembly; from her breach with Duarte's Christian Democrats to her frequent arrests and constant harassment by
security forces; from her collaboration and friendship with
Archbishop Romero to her dedication to the cause of human
rights and her death: Marianella's whole existence traced an

ascending path within the common adventure of liberation and rescue on El Salvador's harsh soil. (Raniero la Valle and Linda Bimbi, *Marianella e i suoi fratelli; una storia latino-americano*. Milan 1983)

Autumn 1984
At last a brief prophetic message. I cannot help being reminded of the times of Francis of Assisi.

At the doors of the church of La Palma in El Salvador the government leaders of that tortured country, homeland of the martyred Archbishop Romero, and the guerrilla leaders shake hands hoping to come to an understanding and make peace.

Beside them three bishops and the papal nuncio stand witnesses to the event, by their presence appealing in the name of all Christians for reconciliation and peace.

Joy fills a people exhausted by war, bathed in blood and poverty, dreaming of justice.

I gaze into the crowd, and far far away, hidden among the least of them I see as in a vision the massive figure of Archbishop Oscar Arnulfo Romero. In his hands he holds the chalice with which he was celebrating that last mass cut short by the bullets of his murderers.

Close by I seem to see the tiny figure of Marianella García with her piercing eyes. She does not hold the priestly chalice. But the torture to which she has been subjected has reduced her to one great clot of blood. Both of them – the martyred bishop and the lamb of his flock – radiate joy and great confidence.

Plainly their martyred bodies were not an obstacle to expressing the happiness won by giving themselves to the people they loved to the final sacrifice.

I gaze at the archbishop who gazes back at me through thick, blood-spattered spectacles. He nods towards Marianella. Carlo, he seems to say, don't talk about me. Our Christian martyrology, thank God, has plenty of bishops on the roll. We bishops must be prepared for martyrdom the moment we become shepherds of the flock, for Jesus himself has said, 'the good shepherd is one who lays down his life for his sheep', when he sees the wolf coming (John 10:11).

But talk about Marianella, please. You see, the time has come when the Church emphasizes to all, especially to women, that they too have a priesthood. All can offer themselves to the Father as victims with Jesus.

Isn't this so?

Do you believe this?

Yes, father, I believe it. Marianella seems very close to me with all that enthusiasm of hers for the Church Militant, for justice for the poor.

She and I were birds of a feather. When I read what she did, I might be reading about what I did in a previous generation.

But more than I, more than we, Father Romero, Marianella was able to put her convictions into practice.

She did not take her faith lightly. She was not satisfied with words.

She was truly cut out for martyrdom.

How I envy her in my weakness!

And what a lot she had to say to my generation, characterized by laziness and permissiveness, in courageously living her faith; in making her prayer not a flight towards sterile middle-class intimism, but a rush to service, to heroism in the defence of the oppressed and the poor!

From her rich boarding school in Spain Marianella very soon abandoned a piety confined only to worship and a comfortable life, to answer the call of history, summoning her to hurry home, where the country people of her martyred land were not only being exploited but tortured, massacred and spirited away forever by death squads, acting on the orders of people whose only religion was the defence of their own unjust interests.

'It is not right!' she would cry – echoing John the Baptist, the prophet of the poor (cf. Matt. 14:4) – to those who slaughtered the peasants of El Salvador on the pretext that they had organized a union.

Marianella the lawyer became the lawyer of the poor, taking up the defence of victims no other lawyer would defend for fear of displeasing the regime.

Nor did she ever retreat, despite threats to her life, reprisals against her family, confiscation of her property and armed assaults on her house, which was reduced to a shambles by marauding soldiers and bandits.

The arrogant feared her. Marianella carried one weapon, a camera, and with it she made available to the world the evidence of the savage torture inflicted by the military on the unarmed masses of the peasantry.

Marianella actually ran the Commission for Human Rights in El Salvador, and despite the threats against her never stopped telling the world what was happening to her country at the hands of those bloodthirsty butchers.

That was Marianella's faith. That was her message to those Christians who habitually evade their responsibilities, whose only talent is for filling churches and holding processions, with never a thought for murderers unpunished and the rights of the poor trampled underfoot and derided.

To silence her, a military interrogator whom she had asked for a glass of water poured a glass of boiling water down her throat, and for good measure stuffed a petrol-soaked rag into her mouth, making her nearly sick with nausea.

But she would not give in. Having left the country, to the great joy of all – her persecutors as well as those who loved and feared for her – she soon found she could not forget the sufferings of her friends and returned to the lion's den, knowing her prospects of being tortured and killed.

And tortured and killed she was.

It was Marianella's good fortune, and El Salvador's good fortune, to have a shepherd like Archbishop Romero.

Timid, accused of being a traditionalist, publicity-shy, scarcely the type to make history, he was not content with saying what is normally said: 'I am the bishop of everyone, I am neutral.'

No, he spoke out boldly against the outrages of the military.

He was not content with saying: 'It isn't my business.' He had the courage, timid as he was by nature, to say to some soldiers who had come to ask his counsel because their consciences were uneasy about firing on unarmed peasants:

'The command, "You shall not kill", must prevail over any

command to kill. No soldier is obliged to obey an order that is against the law of God. An immoral law entails no obligation to obey it.'

How brave!

What if all the Christians in history had observed this maxim of Archbishop Oscar Arnulfo Romero?

What if all today's Christians at once were to deal with the atom bomb in a manner consistent with their faith?

But do you not see, Romero, that by countermanding an official order you are undermining order itself? Do you not see that you are denouncing a society in which Christians make a permanent compromise between convenience and sloth, and power?

There is nothing for it but to slaughter you like Jesus, who undermined the laws dear to the Temple. Yes, slaughter you in the name of law and order.

Prepare to die.

The military could have found another moment but they did not. He had spoken as a bishop, they killed him as a bishop.

During the offertory at mass.

How lucky you were, Archbishop Romero!

Your example helps us change our lives.

For us you are a symbol of the faith lived with courage.

Your example can help us change our lives.

And you too, little Marianella, you are lucky!

You succeeded in expressing what you lived. You are woman all the more woman in your sacrifice.

You have made your way into our hearts; with your blood shed for love you have entered the kingdom of infinite life.

Martyrdom has the primacy over all; you have taken the kingdom by storm.

Baptized before you could know with a little water in your parish church in El Salvador, you have been rebaptized in your own blood in defence of the poor and oppressed of your land.

You too, like your archbishop, can help us to change our lives, and have courage in the faith.

Second day

I love your palace . . .
my king and my God.   (Ps. 84:1,3)

CONTEMPLATION

Pilgrimage Song

How I love your palace,
   Yahweh Sabaoth!
How my soul yearns and pines
   for Yahweh's courts!
My heart and my flesh sing for joy
   to the living God.

The sparrow has found its home at last,
the swallow a nest for its young,
your altars, Yahweh Sabaoth,
   my king and my God.

Happy those who live in your house
   and can praise you all day long;
and happy the pilgrims inspired by you
   with courage to make the Ascents!

As they go through the Valley of the Weeper,
   they make it a place of springs,
clothed in blessings by early rains.
Thence they make their way from height to height,
soon to be seen before God on Zion.

Yahweh Sabaoth, hear my prayer,
listen, God of Jacob;
God our shield, now look on us
and be kind to your anointed.

A single day in your courts
   is worth more than a thousand elsewhere;
merely to stand on the steps of God's house
   is better than living with the wicked.

For God is battlement and shield,
    conferring grace and glory;
Yahweh withholds nothing good
    from those who walk without blame.

Yahweh Sabaoth,
happy the man who puts his trust in you!   (Ps. 84)

1 PETER 1:3–12

JOHN 12:20–6

Benedetta

Hope in Sickness

Benedetta Bianchi Porro, born 8 August 1936 in Dovadola
near Forli, died 23 January 1964 in Sirmione near Brescia.

Stricken with polio when she was only a few months old,
Benedetta attended school only intermittently. At the age of
seventeen she enrolled in the Medical School of the University
of Milan. By now she was growing deaf and this caused her
many humiliations but she tenaciously persisted in her
studies. Deafness was followed by blindness then by total
paralysis. Her illness was diagnosed as advanced neurofibromatosis. On this Calvary Benedetta discovered God's plan
for her, and that 'for those who believe, everything is a sign'.
She became an ambassadress of the Gospel by her life and
voluminous correspondence, dictated to her mother. (*Oltre il
silenzio: diary-letters of Benedetta Bianchi Porro*, collected by Anna
Maria Cappelli. Milan 1983)

Yes, we must act as though everything depended on
ourselves, as St Ignatius says, but then surrender ourselves
as though everything depended on God. And Benedetta
surrendered herself. No easy thing. No easy thing when
self-surrender means accepting the ridicule of our deafness,
and the inability to communicate with those we love and

who love us. None the less she surrenders herself to the dream of a God who will take her in his arms and make her happy. (Carlo Carretto, Preface to *Diary of Benedetta*. Brescia 1984)

Today for many people Benedetta Bianchi Porro is just another name.

We know that she was born in the Romagna, that she was stricken with polio when only a few months old, and that the village children called her Zoppetta (Little Cripple) from the time she could walk.

She moved to Sirmione del Garda to a little villa on the lake, with green shutters, a wooden porch and, as she would say later, 'a feeling of freedom'.

It was to be shortlived, as she was to wear an uncomfortable surgical corset and was aware that, gradually but inexorably, she was going deaf.

'The success of things, the festival of life' was dying within her.

Benedetta came to know the icy cold of naked love, the fear of the void. And she called for help.

Her help came 'from others', sufferers like herself, who lived as she did; from friends; but most of all from the notion that she ought to find a way of doing something for everyone else. She decided to become a doctor – to 'live, struggle and sacrifice for everyone' – and enrolled, with a courage one might call a little mad, in the Medical School in Milan.

Yes, she must have been a bit mad. At the oral examination at the end of her first two years, anxious to make sure she had understood the question put by one of the professors, she put her hand to her ear and asked him to repeat it; whereupon he flung her paper into a corner with the acid words, 'And who ever heard of a deaf doctor?'

Deafness was only the beginning of it. Neurofibromatosis, which was soon to devastate her beautiful young body, was already at work. She was to go blind, lose the sense of touch, and be paralysed, first in her legs and then gradually throughout her whole body.

But let us listen to what she has to say, replying to a letter which a young man who was ill had written to the newspaper *Epoca* in a desperate search for help. Benedetta wrote:

Sirmione 1963
Dear Natalino

There's a letter of yours in *Epoca*. My mother read it to me by touching hands. I'm deaf and blind, so we have to do things the hard way.

Like you, I am twenty-six and have been sick for some time. A disease shrivelled me up just as I was about to complete long years of study. I was about to graduate in medicine in Milan. I had been complaining of deafness for some time but even the doctors didn't believe me at first. So I plunged ahead with my studies, which I was absolutely crazy about, even though I knew the doctors were wrong. I was only seventeen when I started at university.

Then my sickness stopped me cold, just when I'd nearly finished my studies. I was taking my last exam. And the only thing my 'almost-degree' was good for was self-diagnosis, since until then no one had been able to decide what was the matter with me.

Until three months ago I still had fairly good vision. But now all is dark. I'm not hopeless here on my Calvary, though. I know Jesus is waiting for me at the end of the road.

To begin with I lived in a big chair, but now I have to stay in bed. Here I have found a wisdom greater than that of mankind. I've found that there is a God, and that he is love, faithfulness, joy and certainty, even to the end of the world.

Before long I shall be no more than a name. But my spirit will live on here among my family, and among those who suffer; even I shall not have suffered in vain.

Natalino, don't feel alone. Never. Go calmly on down the path of time, and you'll receive light, truth. This is the road where there's really a righteousness, not the righteousness of men and women but the righteousness that God alone can give.

My days are not easy. They're hard. But they're sweet

because Jesus is with me in my suffering. He comforts me in my loneliness and lightens my darkness.

He smiles at me and lets me work with him. So long, Natalino. Life is short. It passes in a flash. Life is a very short bridge: dangerous for people who want to get all the enjoyment out of it they can, but safe for those who cooperate with Jesus to reach our Homeland.

All love,
Your sister in Christ
Benedetta

This letter is a masterpiece. It says everything. Something we can read slowly over and over again when we are confined to bed.

We can hardly be in sadder case, unable to communicate and imprisoned in the cocoon of our suffering. And this is when Benedetta's words will count:

I've found that there is a God, and that he is love, faithfulness, joy and certainty, even to the end of the world. . . .

My days are not easy. They're hard. But they're sweet because Jesus is with me in my suffering. He comforts me in my loneliness and lightens my darkness.

He smiles at me and lets me work with him.

'He lets me work with him.' We could be hearing a letter from Paul, '. . . in my own body . . . I . . . make up all that has still to be undergone by Christ' (Col. 1:24).

It is not easy to speak like this when you are being eaten alive by pain. But this is the only 'emergency exit'. This is my only opportunity to escape the unbearable fact; I toss it into the furnace of love like so much dry tinder.

This is the furnace that moves the stars, this is the furnace that gives life. This is the furnace that saves man, this is the furnace that makes me blessed in the vision of the kingdom.

And this is the furnace that makes us completely aware of the meaning of what Benedetta once said; it even makes us able to say it with her:

As for myself, I live the way I always did and feel perfectly fulfilled . . . and I think of it as a miracle and I should be able to raise a hymn of praise to the One who has given me life. . . . At times I wonder whether I am not one of those creatures to whom much has been given and of whom much will be asked.

How brave!
And again:

In the sorrow of my blindness, in the deep darkness of my solitude, I have tried, willing myself to be serene, to make my sorrow blossom; and thus I seek the humble will to succeed in being as God wishes me: very tiny, as I sincerely believe myself to be, when I manage to see his stupendous grandeur in the dark night of my weary days.

Often she would sing this Negro spiritual to herself:

Sometimes I feel like a motherless child,
Sometimes I feel like an eagle in flight.
Some bright beautiful morning
I'm gonna lay down my burden, spread my wings and
   take the air.
You can bury me in the East,
You can bury me in the West,
But that morning
The angels'll open their big wings
And I'm gonna hear them holy trumpets sound.

And in her search for God she would say:

The days fly by as I wait for the One I love. He is in the air, in the sun I cannot see any more but whose heat I still feel when it comes through the window to warm my hands, and in the rain that comes down from heaven to work the earth.

And when she felt that she was nearing the goal:

Mother, you know that for most people Benedetta is dead already. All the same, many will remember me. The end is near, Mother, but you must never feel alone. I am leaving you so many sons, so many daughters to look after.

. . . I have to tell you – I have already heard the Bridegroom's voice. I'm not very good at praying now. But I offer everything, just as I am. May the One who has been begotten in me guide me to the end.

And us too, with Benedetta, celebrating our sacrifice when we reach the hour of our death.

Third day

Life to me, of course, is Christ, but then death would bring
me something more . . .   (Phil. 1:21)

Lament

Save me, God! The water
  is already up to my neck!
I am sinking in the deepest swamp,
  there is no foothold;
I have stepped into deep water
  and the waves are washing over me.

Worn out with calling, my throat is hoarse,
my eyes are strained, looking for my God.

More people hate me for no reason
  than I have hairs on my head,
more are groundlessly hostile
  than I have hair to show.
(They ask me to give back what I never took.)

God, you know how foolish I have been,
my offences are not hidden from you;

but let those who hope in you not blush for me,
  Yahweh Sabaoth!
Let those who seek you not be ashamed of me,
  God of Israel!

It is for you I am putting up with insults
that cover me with shame,
that make me a stranger to my brothers,
an alien to my mother's other sons;
zeal for your house devours me,
  and the insults of those who insult you fall on me.

If I mortify myself with fasting,
they make this a pretext for insulting me;
if I dress myself in sackcloth,
I become their laughing-stock,
the gossip of people sitting at the city gate,
and the theme of drunken songs.

For my part, I pray to you, Yahweh,
   at the time you wish;
in your great love, answer me, God,
   faithful in saving power.

Pull me out of this swamp; let me sink no further,
   let me escape those who hate me,
   save me from deep water!
Do not let the waves wash over me,
   do not let the deep swallow me
or the Pit close its mouth on me.

In your loving kindness, answer me, Yahweh,
in your great tenderness turn to me;
do not hide your face from your servant,
quick, I am in trouble, answer me;
come to my side, redeem me,
from so many enemies ransom me.

You know all the insults I endure,
every one of my oppressors is known to you;
the insults have broken my heart,
my shame and disgrace are past cure;
I had hoped for sympathy, but in vain,
I found no one to console me.

They gave me poison to eat instead,
when I was thirsty they gave me vinegar to drink.

May their own table prove a trap for them,
and their plentiful supplies, a snare!
may their eyes grow dim, go blind,
strike their loins with chronic palsy!

Vent your fury on them,
let your burning anger overtake them;
may their camp be reduced to ruin,
and their tents left unoccupied:
for hounding a man after you had struck him,
for adding more wounds to those which you inflicted.

Charge them with crime after crime,
deny them further access to your righteousness,
blot them out of the book of life,
strike them off the roll of the virtuous.

For myself, wounded wretch that I am,
by your saving power, God, lift me up!
I will praise the name of God with a song,
I will extol him with my thanksgiving,
more pleasing to Yahweh than any ox
or bull with horn and hoof.

Then, seeing this, the humble can rejoice:
long life to your hearts, all you who seek for God!
Yahweh will always hear those who are in need,
will never scorn his captive people.
Let heaven and earth acclaim him,
the oceans and all that moves in them!

For God will save Zion,
and rebuild the towns of Judah:
they will be lived in, owned,
handed down to his servants' descendants,
and lived in by those who love his name.   (Ps. 69)

1 CORINTHIANS 1:1–31; 2:1–2

MARK 8:34–8

Veronica

The Folly of the Cross

Veronica Giuliani, born 1660 at Mercatello in the Marches. At seventeen she entered the Capuchin convent at Città di Castello, Umbria, where she spent the rest of her life. She died on Friday, 9 July 1727.

The programme of her spiritual life was 'to suffer for love', and her goal, an 'ever greater conformity to Christ crucified'. Her love for his passion earned her the sacred stigmata. Transverberation of the heart and the experience of the 'folly of the cross' caused her physical pain, mental suffering, diabolic temptations, interior struggles and long periods of aridity. She recounted her high mystical experiences in a diary written by order of her confessor. Appropriately Veronica has been declared 'teacher *par excellence* of the doctrine of expiation'. Many requests have been made for her to be proclaimed a Doctor of the Church. (*Il mio Calvario, Autobiography of Sr Veronica Giuliani*. Città di Castello 1976)

I must admit, when I open Veronica's diary I often shut it up again pretty quickly, with a feeling of being in the presence of a creature not of this world. Not that the sweetness of her words has been without effect on me – I who am in love with Christ as she was – but it doesn't seem quite normal to say, in all sincerity:

> Bless you, my Lord. I covet nothing but to suffer for your love. Yes, yes, my God. I shall only be content once I am truly crucified with you.

So forcefully to state such a desire does not sound well to modern ears steeped in a music that speaks exclusively of affluence, achievement, satisfaction and the claims of carnal love.

Try to imagine a girl today, used to having everything, trying everything and getting everything, expressing herself like this:

Strike me, torture me, do anything God pleases – I am his and only wish to do his will. Invent every possible torment and I shall use it to love and cling closer to him, and him alone.

Or this:

My God, I am ready for any pain. . . . This is not the time for resting but for suffering. . . . Lord, I shall not stop scourging myself as long as souls are not converted to you!

What made me think of Veronica's diary again were the drug addicts. Today I seem to be surrounded by them, listening to them, and above all witnessing in them the defeat of modern man. Humanity destroyed by pleasure.

People whose backbone has gone so soft with affluence that they can no longer stand on their two feet.

I could never have believed pleasure to be so dangerous.

Pleasure is a creature of God, the joy of living, strength in weariness, healthy appetite, rapture in love, balm in friendship, rest in fatigue. In a word, it is good, very good!

But ill-sought, sought within myself, detached from the end to which it was bestowed on mankind, it becomes a genuine peril, especially in an age of consumerism such as ours, where, however vitiated and distorted, it can be obtained for money like any nasty drug. When people are poor and hard-working, but rich in ideals and feelings, pleasure is regulated by need and is a true, valid and valuable help.

But when people are rich and grown old in the exercise of power, strangers to nature and wholesome toil, with no obstacle or limit to their desires, pleasure eventually becomes genuinely dangerous.

There is no limit to the havoc it can wreak in people with no ideals, bored, rich, arrogant and without the one brake which could be useful, with its eternal challenge – God.

That is why drugs have claimed and are claiming so many victims. And the worst of it is, they will claim innumerable more.

Mankind itself seems in danger, and I fear for its future.

The slope down which we are sliding is a fearful one since at its bottom awaits mankind's ugliest temptation: slow suicide.

Suicide by pleasure. We are too conditioned by our senses; and pleasure makes us like drunkards on a greasy pole.

There is nothing for it but to roll to the very bottom. And we shall tumble all the faster since the moral climate – let us not mince words – is putrid.

We are in a climate of collapse, of the end of the empire; of moral dissolution in which the most radical crisis has surfaced, attacking everything and everyone, the state, the school, the party, the family, the individual.

And why was it precisely drug addicts that inspired me to open Veronica's diary again? I had come back from a Congress of Rehabilitation Centres, where administrators, medical tutors and psychologists had talked at great length on the methods they found most effective for helping addicts who were trying to kick the habit and escape from the diabolical spiral of drug dependency.

All were agreed on the need to find ideals capable of stirring the victim's diseased will. All were convinced that a way would have to be found of offering the patient some means – harsh if necessary but voluntarily accepted – of strengthening a will weakened by vice.

That night I was unable to sleep, so I opened Veronica's book. It was given to me by the Capuchin Father Indovino, who is deeply in love with this saintly person.

And I read:

Would you be saved? Embrace the cross. By suffering you will find the strength to be converted to the joy of living. Leave, leave the false delights of the world and come with me. You will find freedom and love.

Look at that, I said to myself. Why, I should put this maniac Veronica in charge of a rehabilitation centre without a second thought. She would soon heal other maniacs like her.

Drug addicts are drugged on madness. They need someone,

someone drugged on love, like her, to pull them out of it; better still, to get them to switch drugs.

Basically it would be so simple. All they would need to do would be to switch drugs. The love drug would beat the pleasure drug.

When someone is mad anything is worth trying. Now I understand the folly of the cross. May God give it to me too!

Surely there could be no more effective therapy for someone sunk in lust, debauchery or sloth, someone immersed in the good life. Which of us has never felt the value of the pilgrim's sack, the strength that comes from fasting, the efficacity of penance preached by saints to deliver us from the thrall of idols; from the fraud inherent in a middle-class life remote from the ideal of the kingdom and the incalculable worth of service?

We know all this, of course. What struck me in the case of Veronica was more particularly the madness. This is the indispensable element for any therapy of our own, refined as we may be thanks to television and technology.

As a matter of fact, whenever I have had the luck to make some converts I have always noticed an increased brilliance in their eyes, and heard a strange new tone in their voice.

It is as though they were moving from one madness to another. First, they overdid evil. And now . . .

No, I cannot say that they are overdoing good. But there are clear signs that perfect equilibrium is far to seek. Patience!

I wish I could overdo good, and love; and in particular I wish I could overdo suffering, in so far as is needful to give me victory over my overdone selfishness.

When I hear Veronica say –

Once more it seemed to me that the desire for suffering had been kindled in my heart and I then experienced more interior peace.

Henceforth I cared for nothing. In this life everything filled me with disgust, and I repeated again and again, with my St Paul: 'I want to be gone and be with Christ!' (Phil. 1:23)

– I cannot fail to see that Jesus himself was the first to bear the folly of the cross on earth, and that this supreme madness can fall like a sledge-hammer on the hard heart of man, however imprisoned in sensual pleasure he may be, and smash it.

'Henceforth I cared for nothing. In this life everything filled me with disgust.'

This affirmation is a victory for man imprisoned in self and unable to escape the hell of selfishness. To find the strength to break free!

At last, the strength to free ourselves, to come out of ourselves singing for joy.

'My strength is the Lord. Forever is he Israel's saviour.'

The violent wrench that a loving acceptance of pain can give is often the only way left by which to escape the hell of vice. The folly of throwing ourself into the brambles, as Francis did to overcome sensual temptation, is wisdom in whoever can grasp the point.

Not for nothing did Jesus say, 'If your hand or your foot should cause you to sin, cut it off and throw it away. . . . And if your eye should cause you to sin, tear it out . . .' (Matt. 18:8–9; cf. Mark 9:43–7).

This is the folly of the cross, demanding me to sacrifice hand and eye! But this is still not enough, for love helps me to will all.

Veronica says:

One day a certain feeling came over me that I could not well understand. I hurried back to my cell but found no relief there. I said within myself, 'My Jesus, what do you wish me to do? I hear you calling but cannot see you.' As I said this, I had another feeling. I felt as it were a flame in my heart that set me ablaze. I hurried to the church and with all my heart I said, 'Here I am, ready for everything; only tell me what you want of me.' As I said this I felt myself to be all fire. I could not control myself. Now I ran, now I sang, now I was struck dumb, but all I could hear was an interior voice inviting me to suffer.

Yes, if I could find someone like Veronica, that would be the one to put in charge of a rehabilitation centre for drug addicts.

And if there was another to be found of the same mettle, that's who I would put in charge of the world's alcoholics.

And if I found a third, that's who I would invite to my community of Little Brothers to teach us how to gain a maturity like that.

'Now I ran, now I sang, now I was struck dumb, but all I could hear was an interior voice inviting me to suffer.'

What incredible freedom you can gain from victory over pleasure and acceptance of the cross for love of the kingdom!

And for service to our fellow-men. And for confronting life as we find it. And for curing our habitual whining. And for learning the joy of singing in the sun. And being happy to be alive. And for being unafraid to die.

And for giving our days a meaning. And for defeating the evil one. And for feeling a little crazy; as she did, Veronica Giuliani.

Appendix: Woe to the Solitary!

I thought it would be a good idea to add a note on *community of faith and prayer*, and *community of life*.

Too many Christians still undervalue the importance of the community as a means towards the systematic development of our faith.

Scripture says, 'woe to the man by himself' (Eccles 4:10; cf. Gen. 2:18).

This is a serious warning. It says: Be warned, solitude can hurt you.

Just imagine what might happen when you are suffering, when you are old, when you are in a crisis!

We ought to think about this; we ought to look ahead to the years which old age can turn into tragedy.

We must all have a community.

We must seek it out, prepare it and make it live, creating a constant climate of help, friendship and prayer.

Consider the tragic fate of the elderly completely deserted in their loneliness, bored to tears, never receiving visits, passing hour after hour without the joys of friendship.

The fault may lie with others, in the prevailing climate of selfishness.

But then again, it may not.

What did *you* do when you were young and able to break the vicious circle of loneliness?

Were you concerned about others?

Or were you satisfied with enjoying your health and personal freedom?

There are some, especially among the rich and well-to-do,

who do not prepare wisely for old age; who are content to say, 'People should keep to themselves.'

Of course, rich people's flats are always double-locked, and often enough people in the same block do not know one another.

The poor in small villages are wiser. They live out of doors. They can hear their neighbours' voices. Their doors are open to all.

Women and children constantly run in and out of each other's houses exchanging greetings and news.

The poor are much wiser. They prepare for old age.

They are not often alone and for them old age is more bearable.

In contrast . . . how sad a rich man's home is, double-locked, with some old party completely alone inside!

But there is more to it than this, something very important.

The Bible's 'woe to the man by himself' is a serious valuable warning for true Christians, especially today.

It is a call to all who seek to live their faith and make it effective in life.

Jesus founded the Church precisely for this purpose. The Church is the answer to our need for communion and assistance.

But we must not be content with any old church, with one that by sheer weight of numbers becomes incapable of responding to our needs.

How can you get help from ten, twenty, thirty thousand people?

What can you get from a nameless mass of people you do not know, among whom there is no exchange, no talk?

No, the parish population should be divided into small communities, real communities in which people will actually know one another, will discover common interests and have the wherewithal to make a common journey.

The community should be of manageable dimensions, such as Boy Scouts, Catholic Action, Neo-Catechumenal Way, charismatic renewal groups, and other prayer meetings.

And if I do not like the existing organizations I shall start others more suited to my needs. The main thing is for these communities to live by faith, the word of God, and friendship, great friendship.

Everyone ought to belong to such a fellowship, especially the youth and the elderly; and often enough our own home is the best place for Christian prayer and fellowship groups to meet.

To put it another way: we ought to be building up the local church.

The council helped us rediscover the role of the bishop with his clergy and their piece of the church.

At grass-roots level is where, since its beginnings, the Church's most valuable experiences have been acquired.

And perhaps the days of large congregations are over; in them the notion of fellowship was more of a theory than a fact.

What we are beginning to see today is the need for religious communities grouped around the bishop and expressing the charisms of various churches.

I feel very fortunate in that, in the church in which I have grown old, I have seen just such an experiment in progress.

I should like to say something to you about the Jesus Caritas Community.

It was founded in 1969 in Umbria, that luminous land of Benedict of Nursia and Francis of Assisi.

Today it numbers some twenty sisters and brothers living the contemplative missionary ideal of Charles de Foucauld in small fraternities, and devoting themselves to prayer and evangelization, in close collaboration with the local church.

Their prior has written:

Though reaching here by different routes, we can all practically touch the mystery of God's love, and we live in community 'for the sake of Jesus and the Gospel' to serve the local church, and hence to be part of the civil community.

Our vocation is one of adoration, praise, work and service.

We are contemplatives in solidarity, we testify that Jesus is alive, that he has come and that he will come again. We are little monks and little nuns living as sisters and brothers, as we would in everyday life.

Our ordained brothers have been entrusted by our bishop with a parish, and naturally our community of brothers and sisters lives as part of this canonical community.

We sing the divine office, we read the Bible, we worship in silence, from dawn to dusk.

In the *Directorium* of the community – its brief Rule – we read:

For the community to be a true one, each of the brothers and sisters is to foster an interior spirit of contemplation, through a living participation in the liturgy, that 'source and summit of the life of the Church', in the celebration of the Eucharist, in regular and prolonged adoration, and in meditation on the word of God, thereby transforming the entire day into an incessant hymn of praise.

In the spirit of monasticism throughout the ages Jesus Caritas practises hospitality and simple sharing. The prior explains:

It is not so much a matter of keeping the doors of our houses physically open. This goes without saying, as our houses are canonically erected and therefore open to the people of God.

The important thing is to open our houses to the poorest of the poor, to bring them peace, hope and serenity, and so be evangelized by them in our turn.

A large part of the day is reserved for work:

Our work is guided by the following criteria. It must be useful. It must be prayerful. It must be well done, in love and poverty. It must be witness. Finally it must be balanced and real. . . . We must not evade the law of toil. This would be a serious sin, a gross breach of our duty to identify ourselves with our fellow-men.

In a word, we must take the Incarnation seriously.

Nearly seventy years after the death of Father de Foucauld on 1 December 1916, I, one of his Little Brothers, rejoice that the seed buried in the sandy soil of Tamanrasset in the Sahara continues generating men and women to serve the Church, whatever form their consecration may take, in total self-surrender to the Father, imitating Jesus of Nazareth in their overriding commitment to 'proclaim the Gospel with their lives'.

Other Orbis Titles . . .

by Carlo Carretto

I, FRANCIS

"Here is an imagined 'autobiography' of the saint from Assisi that is both inventive and poetic. In a style by turns whimsical, rapturous, innocent, canny, and wise we are given descriptions of Francis' pampered childhood, his vision of 'Lady Poverty' and youthful escapades as a sort of local Robin Hood, his call to 'repair {God's} house,' his subsequent path of radical poverty, and the growth of his order."   *Library Journal*

no. 200-0   **144pp. pbk.**   **$6.95**

SUMMONED BY LOVE

A sustained meditation based on a prayer of Charles deFoucauld known as the *Prayer of Abandonment*.

"This valuable and timely book offers encouragement and challenge for all seeking to live within the changing Church to find hope and love therein."   *Catholic Library World*

no. 472-0   **143pp. pbk.**   **$5.95**

LETTERS FROM THE DESERT

Writing for his fellow Christians, Carlo Carretto shares his beautiful and powerful expressions of faith.

"*Letters From the Desert* contains seventeen letters, some in the form of brief meditations on such topics as Purification of the Heart, The Stages of Prayer, Contemplative Prayer and Purification of the Spirit, and others that are simply personal accounts of his life as a novice."

Homiletic and Pastoral Review

no. 280-9   **146pp. pbk.**   **$5.95**

I SOUGHT AND I FOUND

Carlo Carretto's spiritual biography. In it he sums up his religious experience over a long life, from his peasant childhood, through his life in the Sahara to his more recent experiences as a spiritual director. He speaks of faith, hope and love with devasting honesty and simplicity.

no. 202-7   **144pp. pbk.**   **$6.95**

BLESSED ARE YOU WHO BELIEVED

The devotional reflections that Carlo Carretto offers here record how he came to consider Mary "the sister of my heart, the companion of my pilgrimage, my teacher in faith."

"An unusual little book which takes the form of a free-form meditation on the trials and tribulations experienced by Mary during her pregnancy."

U.S. Catholic

no. 038-5   **96pp. pbk.**   **$4.95**

THE GOD WHO COMES

"A gem from Carlo Carretto. In this book he shares the magnificent Catholic reflections that have inspired him. He tells, for instance, of spending days alone in a cave, alone, that is, with Christ in the Eucharist. His reflections are tremendous; that's the only word strong enough to describe them."

The Priest

no. 160-8   **254pp. pbk.**   **$6.95**

LOVE IS FOR LIVING

A journey of meditation through the Bible.

"These meditations are serious—serious about the Bible, serious about the condition of modern people, and serious about the position the church occupies in the contemporary world. There is no sugarcoating, no easy sentimentality. When answers are proposed, they are never simple or enticing. When Carretto speaks of "sweetness" it is in conjunction with the strength that God gives. A phrase the author uses could describe the effect of the book: attentive, dynamic, virile and passionate."

no. 293-0   **158pp. pbk.**   **$5.95**

by Joseph G. Donders

JESUS, THE STRANGER
Reflections on the Gospels

This collection of free-flowing sermons is divided into six main groups paralleling the period of Jesus Christ's life.

". . . brilliantly unfolds the pleasures of the salvation and blessed intoxication the very name of Jesus clearly represents. Here is a remarkable original presentation, a rare growing experience for the reader, a powerful message that will be bathed in its own priority and light on your bookshelf long after many other books have lost their glow."

Religious Book Review

no. 235-3   **290pp. pbk.**   **$8.95**

THE PEACE OF JESUS
Reflections on the Gospel for the A-Cycle

A book of reflections based on the Sunday gospels of the A-year of the liturgical cycle. The author writes the stories of the Gospel in colloquial and contemporary language, provides angles of insight on familiar passages and nudges toward human need on our scene.

"Many a writer has attempted to describe Jesus' message of love and compassion only to find it often defies translation. In Donders' case much of that joy is communicable."   *Religious Book Review*

no. 379-1   **213pp. pbk.**   **$9.95**

BEYOND JESUS
Reflections on the Gospel for the B-Cycle

Beyond Jesus is more than a collection of meditations for the B-Cycle. It is a journey in faith that oscillates between the first-century world of Jesus and his followers and the realities of twentieth century existence. The result is a Jesus relevant for our time. Written in poetic, story-like fashion, *Beyond Jesus* is a compelling resource for all Christians seeking to relate the gospel to today's individual and social needs. Excellent for sermons and personal devotions.

no. 049-0   **304pp. pbk.**   **$10.95**

by Dom Helder Camara

HOPING AGAINST ALL HOPE

Prose and poetry from the Brazilian archbishop internationally known for his advocacy of the poor and oppressed.

"There are few people around the world who keep going—and help keep others going—hoping against hope. Dom Helder is one of these. He combines, in a unique way, intense suffering and a spirit of joyous abandon."   *Richard Schaull*

no. 192-6   **96pp. pbk.**   **$4.95**